THE BROKEN COLUMN

By the same authors:

ABOVE US THE WAVES

WILL NOT WE FEAR

THE ADMIRALTY REGRETS . .

C. E. T. WARREN and JAMES BENSON

The Broken Column

The story of James Frederick Wilde's
adventures with the Italian partisans

WHITE LION PUBLISHERS
London, New York, Sydney and Toronto

First published in the United Kingdom by
George G. Harrap Ltd., 1966

White Lion edition, 1975

ISBN 0 85617 678 8

Printed in Great Britain by
Biddles Ltd., Guildford, Surrey,
for White Lion Publishers Ltd.,
138 Park Lane, London W1Y 3DD

Authors' Note

ALTHOUGH this is the story of James Frederick Wilde and his adventures with the Italian partisans, it could not be based exclusively upon his own recollections. There was a great deal of which he was unaware: the motives behind certain actions, for example, as well as those events at which he was not present, yet which form an integral part of his story.

This book is in part the result of retracing Wilde's journey, of talking to the people who helped him while he was on the run and fought with him in the mountains. We hope that it thus has an entity it would not otherwise have possessed, and that this note explains the presence in the text of certain incidents about which Wilde must clearly have been ignorant at the time.

Contents

Plates

between pages 104 & 105

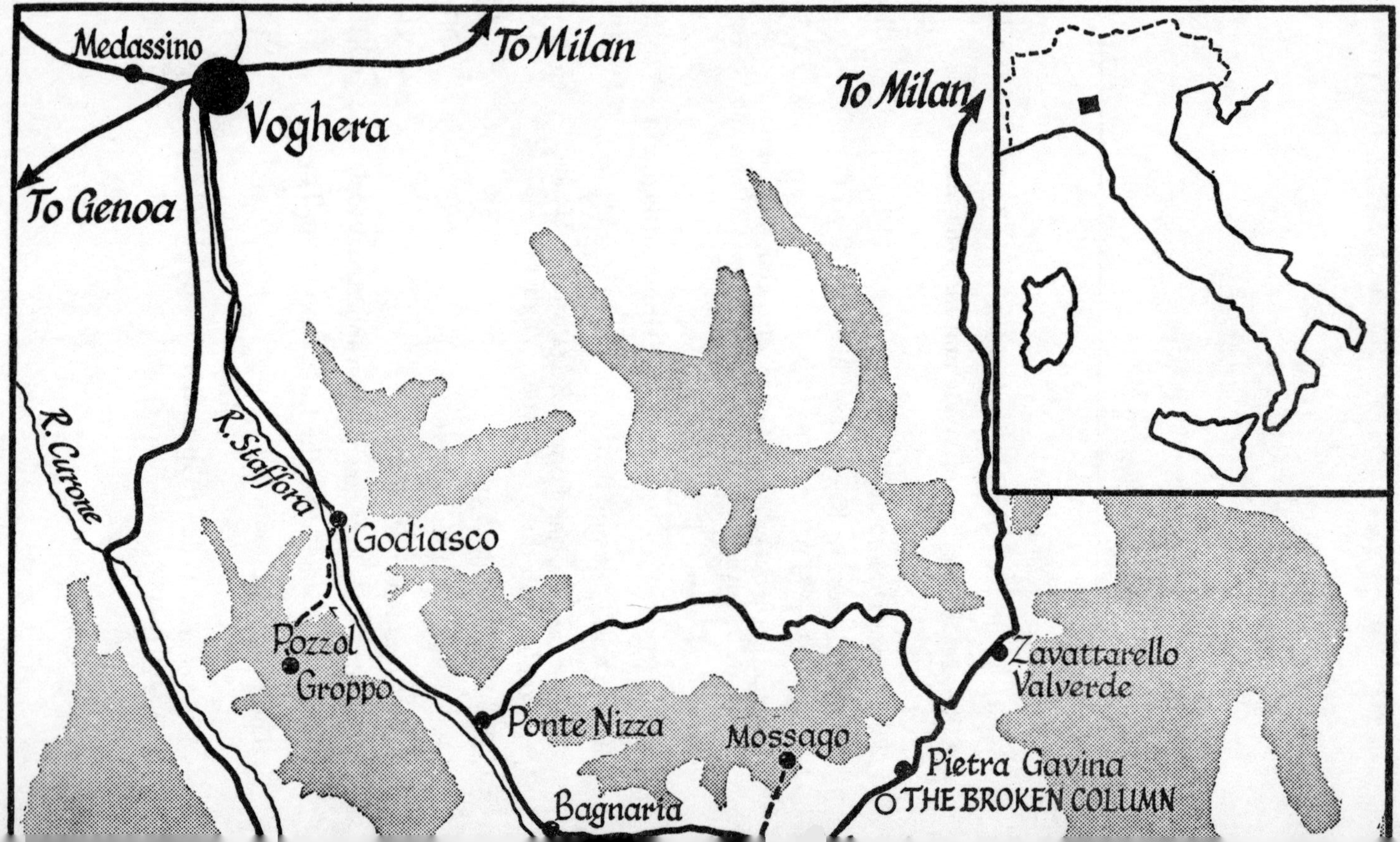
Medassino
Voghera
To Milan
To Milan
To Genoa
R. Curone
R. Staffora
Godiasco
Pozzol
Groppo
Ponte Nizza
Mossago
Bagnaria
Zavattarello
Valverde
Pietra Gavina
THE BROKEN COLUMN

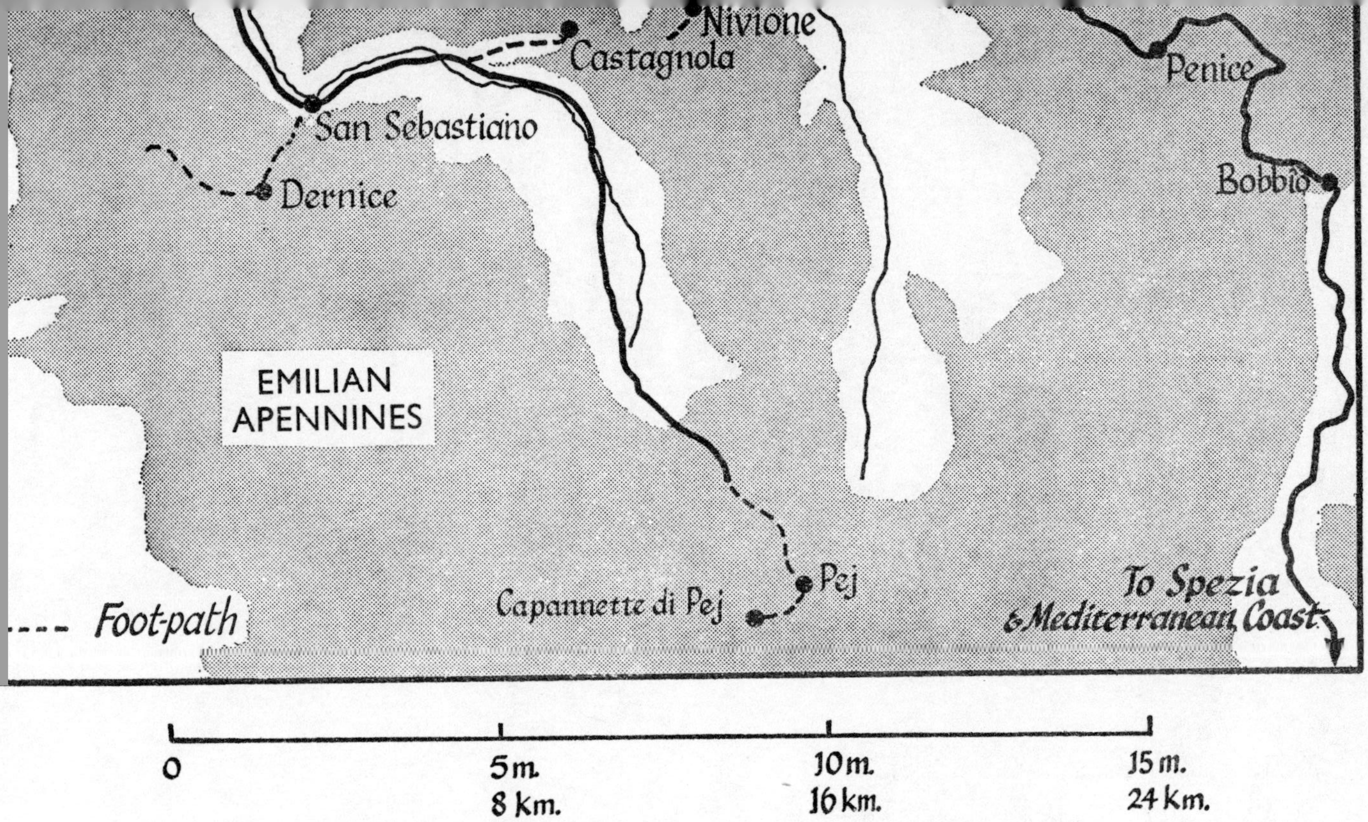

The scene of Wilde's Operations around Voghera and Varzi

Prologue

LATER Wilde was to think that perhaps Minter had been right: that the entire series of events had its origins in the loss of the captain's sunglasses. That, and its being Friday. And, of course, the odd behaviour of the Royal Marine band . . .

All sailors are superstitious, submariners particularly so. A special day of the week, a rabbit's foot, a lucky number, a photograph of a loved one, a medallion, an unexpected change in a regular pattern of behaviour—all have their values and significances, good or evil. And for *Sahib* there was also a collective mascot: the captain's sunglasses. "Butcher" John Bromage's extra-special, lightweight, anti-glare, guaranteed-no-distortion sunglasses were lucky: the crew were convinced of it.

When Bromage dropped them over the side he swore with passionate fluency—and Leading Signalman Minter groaned. "Jim," he said gloomily, "this'll be our last patrol."

Able Seaman James Frederick Wilde shrugged, and then pointed towards the submarine's bridge, where orders and counter-orders were being shouted across the water between *Sahib* and her depot ship, *Maidstone*. Although the submarine was ready for sea, due to sail within the hour, Bromage persuaded *Maidstone* to send down a diver. He made a brief, unsuccessful search for the sunglasses, and at the scheduled time *Sahib*'s propellers churned the filthy waters of Algiers harbour into whiteness as she left on patrol.

"And that's another thing," said Minter. "I never did hold with sailing on a Friday. . . . What's that?"

From the deck of one of the ships in the harbour came the sound of music. A Royal Marine band was 'playing them out', a ceremony usually reserved for one of the big 'uns: an aircraft carrier, a battleship, or a cruiser. It was an honour not previously accorded *Sahib*, and therefore a break from normal routine. Therefore sinister.

Fifteen days later, on Saturday, April 24th, 1943, *Sahib* was still on patrol. She had dived at 5.30 A.M., shortly before dawn. The two off-duty watches had eaten and were trying to sleep; some in bunks, others on piles of clothing, a few in the limited number of hammocks for which there was space in the torpedo compartment. A morning like a hundred others—even when the strident alarm tore the men from their rest and set them running to their diving stations.

A target had been sighted.

James Wilde's action station was alongside numbers one, three, and five torpedo tubes. Since everything depended now upon split-second timing, there was no opportunity to ask questions or expect explanations. That would come later. For the moment Wilde's task was simply to obey the instructions that came over the boat's telephone.

Bromage manœuvred *Sahib* into position and gave the order to fire. As the salvo of torpedoes raced through the sea Wilde counted the seconds and listened hard. After an agony of waiting he heard the loud, reverberating explosion that told him the target had been hit. The crew cheered—and cheered again when Bromage told them over the loudspeaker system that they had sunk an Italian ammunition ship. They were still congratulating themselves when the counter-attack began.

The crew were well accustomed to being depth-charged, but it was clear from the outset that his attack was going to be both heavy and accurate. Charges exploded above and around *Sahib*, making the submarine vibrate and shudder. "In a way that period was worse than anything that followed," Wilde recalls. "Simply waiting, powerless. Unable to hit back. Having to take it . . . Just waiting."

Paint and cork filling showered down from the deckhead. Lampshades crashed to the steel deck. Crockery was smashed, and gear not securely lashed down bounced and slithered around the boat. The men had to hold hard to stanchions and machinery to stay on their feet. Wilde saw a messmate calmly reading a book, and marvelled—until he realized the book was held upside down.

The number of explosions mounted and came closer—until, suddenly, the pressure in the submarine rose. They had been holed. For a few seconds there was absolute silence; then Bromage's voice came over the Tannoy with the order, "Abandon ship!"

"There was no panic," says Wilde, "nor was I scared—although I don't know why not. All I felt, curiously enough, was annoyance at having been told to leave. It seemed ridiculous to suggest *Sahib* was finished."

The submarine stayed on an even keel, and Wilde went aft to the galley where D.S.E.A. (Davis Submarine Escape Apparatus) sets were being issued. Then he heard the order, "Off clips", and even as he looked up towards the gun-tower hatch somebody was opening it. To his intense surprise—and relief—he saw a circle of beautifully clear sky. Despite being holed, *Sahib* had managed to reach the surface on her buoyancy tanks.

When his turn came Wilde pulled himself through the hatchway. Machine-gun bullets from a pair of low-flying German aircraft sprayed the water around *Sahib*, and shells from a group of Italian destroyers were falling dangerously close. Wilde saw Leading Seaman Briard struggling to bring the gun into action and went to help. But a voice yelled, "Get clear of that gun!" and Wilde jumped obediently into the sea. Slowly he swam away from the submarine with a group of other seamen, stokers, and artificers.

The submarine was still making way through the water, widening the gap between herself and the survivors. Wilde wondered why on earth they had abandoned her: she still looked good enough to have had a go at the destroyers. . . . But even as the thought came to him *Sahib* started to sink.

"Three cheers for *Sahib*!" shouted Able Seaman Tinewell. The men cheered. *Sahib* dipped her bows and disappeared.

Wilde could see land on the far horizon, and decided to leave the main body of swimmers and make for it. It occurred to him that being on the loose in enemy Italy offered greater chances of escape than a prison camp. But the destroyers gave him no opportunity of trying. They circled the swimmers, and Wilde trod water until he found himself climbing a scrambling net to the deck of one of the ships. He was followed by Minter and a young seaman who had only recently joined *Sahib*.

The two German aircraft reappeared and machine-gunned the remaining swimmers. As he stood at the destroyer's guard rail shouting curses and shaking his fist at the planes Wilde noticed that a great deal of attention was being paid to the young sailor who had come aboard with Minter. The boy had forgotten to slip off his D.S.E.A set before climbing the scrambling net—and it was well known that the German and Italian navies lacked comparable apparatus. Triumphantly an Italian petty officer lifted the straps from the lad's shoulders and made towards the bridge with the set.

Wilde acted quickly. He stepped forward, and without a word gently took the set from the Italian's hands, walked to the side, and dropped it over. The speed, as well as the audacity, of the action seemed temporarily to mesmerize the petty officer. But before the set hit the water he was himself again—and smashed his fist hard into Wilde's face.

A few minutes later Wilde was paraded before an English-speaking officer. As he had been trained to do, he said only: "My rank is Able Seaman. My number is D/SSX, 29017, and my name is James Frederick Wilde."

Up to this point the life of James Frederick Wilde could be described as ordinary . . . undistinguished . . . average.

He was born in Sheffield on March 31st, 1920, the seventh of eleven children. His father George—nicknamed "Cag"—was a steel-worker. Life was rough and hard for the Wildes. In the industrial North during the nineteen-twenties and early nineteen-thirties a family's income and expenditure were budgeted with extreme care and skill. A penny really mattered, and, while the Wildes were not destitute, such things as holidays were luxuries that happened to other people. The annual highlight of their lives was a day trip to the seaside organized by a local working-men's club.

Worshipped by his family, George Wilde was a devoted gardener who had something of a reputation for his roses. When he could afford it he liked a glass of beer, a ticket for a boxing match, or a visit with his wife to a local cinema. He was a man fanatical about the virtues of hard work and honesty.

His son James, round-faced and slightly built, had only one ambition: to join the Royal Navy. In this he had George's complete approval, and early in 1939 he reported to Devonport Barracks as a seaman recruit. Before his training was complete Britain was at war, and Wilde was drafted to the light cruiser *Ceres*, operating from the Clyde and Scapa Flow. The first months of the War passed without incident. Wilde discovered that he suffered occasionally from seasickness; he tasted his first pint of beer ashore in the Orkneys; and the interest in boxing he inherited from his father led him to become a useful welterweight.

In February 1940 he was back at Devonport taking a three months' course in electrics and torpedoes. He qualified as a seaman-torpedoman, and was drafted to the twenty-year-old destroyer *Broke*. At the time of the fall of France Wilde was one of a party sent ashore to destroy strategic dockyard installations at Brest, and this incident was followed by a series of hazardous escort duties in the North Atlantic. Then, early in 1942, he volunteered for submarines.

"I suppose I volunteered out of some vague sense of patriotism." he says. "They'd announced they were short of submarine crews, so I put my name down. That's all there is to it."

On April 18th, 1942, he was drafted to Birkenhead to join His Majesty's Submarine *P212*, later rechristened *Sahib*. In August she sailed for the Mediterranean, and was soon off on her first patrol: off Corsica. She returned to Malta ten days later with her supply of torpedoes exhausted and a number of small ships to her credit. Some patrols later, during January 1943, *Sahib* achieved the rare distinction of sinking another submarine, *U301*. On the same patrol she also sank an Italian merchantman, but jubilation at this success turned to gloom when, in the process of picking up survivors, it was found that she had been carrying a large number of British prisoners of war. Some were saved, but many drowned.

Sahib's successes continued, from Malta, then Algiers. By now Allied forces in the Mediterranean were both strong and confident, and the general feeling of optimistic expectancy was certainly shared by *Sahib* and her crew—until that Friday morning when the captain's sunglasses went over the side and the Royal Marine band played them out of harbour.

Equally, however, it was the day that set in motion the series of events that was to make James Frederick Wilde anything but ordinary, undistinguished, or average.

Chapter
ONE

Imprisonment and Escape

THE survivors of H.M.S. *Sahib*—six officers and forty-two men—stood huddled together in the dockyard at Messina: exhausted and hungry, their still-damp uniforms clinging to their bodies. Says Wilde: "It was only then, three hours after the sinking, that there came a proper awareness of what had happened—that the boat had gone down, that we were prisoners of war . . . and also that we were incredibly lucky to be alive. Seldom when a submarine was sunk were there survivors. We'd lost only one man, the Chief Electrical Artificer."

During the afternoon they embarked in a small tug and crossed to the mainland where they were issued with distinctively patched Italian army battledress. Then, at six o'clock, the officers were separated from the men, and both groups marched to a railway siding where a train was waiting. Wilde shared a compartment with five other members of the crew and an Italian army corporal. As the train pulled out two other soldiers came round, issuing dry biscuits: one a man. If this was more generous than it may appear—each biscuit was the size of a plate and half an inch thick—it was negated by the fact that the biscuits were as hard as rock and virtually inedible.

There was no glass in the window by which Wilde was sitting, and as the train gathered speed the non-stop blast of cold night air made sleep impossible, despite his dreadful weariness.

They reached Naples in the early morning. As Wilde sat

looking out at the people on the platform a railwayman came along and began making mocking and insulting gestures. "When he spat at me," says Wilde, "I decided enough was enough. I took my biscuit—it was so hard my teeth had only been able to make a few dents in it—and threw it at him with all my strength. It landed across the bridge of his nose with the effect of a large flat stone. Now he really did have something to gesture about."

Grinning, Wilde turned towards his companions—to see a rifle butt coming straight for his face. In the brief second before it hit him Engine Room Artificer Hart grabbed the gun and twisted it from the soldier's hands. Then he handed it back with the warning, "Do that again and I'll wrap it round your bloody neck." Hart's tone of voice and the expression on his face obviated the need for translation. The corporal passed off the incident with a shrug, and such is the unpredictable volatility of the Italian temperament that it was not long before he was singing Neapolitan love ballads to his prisoners. When the train drew out from Naples he produced his lunch—a vast quantity of sandwiches, fruit, and cheese—and shared it among them.

They arrived at Rome at four o'clock that afternoon, and were marched from the main-line station to the terminus of a smaller line. There they were split into two equal groups, and the party with which Wilde found himself was told to board a battered and ramshackle train. When they asked about their shipmates they were assured they would meet them later.

Their journey lasted two hours, until they reached the wayside halt of Manciano. From there they were formed into columns and marched off. "It was a beautiful, warm evening," Wilde recalls. "We forgot how tired we were as we crossed this magnificent countryside, with its woods and fields. Then, after about three-quarters of an hour, I began to grow anxious. I thought that maybe we were being taken to some quiet, out-of-the-way spot to be shot. Then, thank heavens, we saw the villa."

They were now some seventy miles north-west of Rome and

about twenty miles inland, and the building they were approaching was white and elegant, with no sign of barbed wire, sentry boxes, or other symbols of a P.O.W. camp. If this in itself held a suggestion of improbability, their welcome verged on absurdity. They were greeted by an English-speaking Italian captain who was the essence of apologetic solicitude. Would they care to bathe before dining? He was very sorry that they would have to share three bathrooms between them, and that there was not sufficient space to allow for separate bedrooms. . . . Dinner consisted of meat and *pasta*, with a choice of red or white chianti, followed by apples, grapes, and peaches, then coffee and cognac. The very excellence of the meal aroused further suspicions, and Wilde felt that the two warm, clean, neatly folded blankets with which he was issued could easily serve as a shroud.

Then came a dramatic surprise. They found they were sharing the villa with another group of submariners: survivors from *Splendid*. She had been sunk in conditions similar to those of *Sahib*, and the good fortune of Wilde and his comrades was restated when it was learnt that nearly thirty of *Splendid*'s crew had been killed in the depth-charging that blew her to the surface.

One reassurance came from the men of *Splendid*, who had been at the villa for some time: to take conditions at their face value. The *Sahib* men did so, and as the weeks passed Wilde found that his health improved, he put on weight and acquired a deep suntan.

There was a certain amount of cleaning and polishing to be done at the villa, but nobody pretended that it approached hard work. Sometimes, as though to break the monotony, the captain would interrogate them. He invariably apologized for doing so, explaining diffidently that it was a task he found unpleasant, embarrassing, and regrettable. He limited himself to just one question: "What did you do in the submarine?" The rehearsed answer was, "I was a steward for the seamen", or "I was a steward for the stokers", and the captain would sigh, shake his head, and reply, 'Never before have I heard of a submarine run only by stewards."

Every evening he would allow just one senior petty officer to listen to the nine o'clock news from London. Even for this there had to be an apology: more could not listen in case there was a Fascist Party member among his men who would report him. It was over the radio, in June, that the prisoners learned that the island of Pantellaria had surrendered. There was great elation: the Allies seemed poised to invade the Italian mainland, and it would not be long now before they were freed.

Then the Germans arrived.

Their coming was preceded by a lorry piled high with barbed wire and fencing equipment. As it was erected round the villa Wilde reproached himself for not having attempted to escape while he had had the chance. "In a way," he says, "the trouble was that life had been too easy, too quiet. We'd been able to shut our minds to reality and take life as it came, eating and sleeping and sitting in the sun. But the presence of the Germans put an end to all that."

There were two naval officers and six ratings, and their coming created an environment far removed from *opéra bouffe*. The atmosphere was now one of menace and fear, and the first blow came after about ten days: nearly all the *Sahib* and *Splendid* prisoners were shipped to a camp in Germany. A few, however—Wilde among them—stayed behind to help make preparations to receive a new batch of prisoners. When they arrived Wilde found they included the *Sahib* sailors left behind in Rome.

He was delighted to see them—and appalled. Skeletal, dirty, unshaven, they had been housed in a barracks run on strict Fascist lines. On a minimum of food they had been forced to perform a maximum of work under monstrously severe conditions. Typical of them was Wilde's former messmate, Able Seaman Bell. Aboard ship he had weighed fifteen stones: now he had shrunk to less than ten.

"When the Germans left routine went back to normal," says Wilde, "yet it wasn't really the same. I became depressed and broody, speculating on the future, feeling guilty at not taking any more part in the War and at not having escaped, wondering how my family and fiancée, Doreen, were getting on back in Sheffield—I went through a period I once read described as the long black night of the soul. And before I could snap out of it the Germans were back again."

This time there was no waiting. They stayed only the night, and when they left almost the entire complement of prisoners went with them. Now, for the first time, Wilde realized how dominant a determined captor could be. There was to be no singing. . . . No talking after 6 P.M. . . . No use of the lavatory between 6 P.M. and 6 A.M. . . . No lights after 7.30 P.M. . . . No windows to be opened. . . . All blinds drawn immediately a train stopped at a station. They were told: "Any infringement of these rules will be punishable by death. We do not tolerate insubordination in Germany."

It took six days to reach Hamburg, and the journey had been so depressingly monotonous, so rigorous and claustrophobic, that the prisoners were almost looking forward to what lay ahead.

The sentries patrolling the barbed wire, and the bleak wooden watch-towers, allowed for no mistaking the function of the establishment to which they were taken. On arrival they were escorted to the solitary-confinement block in which all new drafts were housed until after their interrogations. The cell in which Wilde was locked contained a double-tier bunk, a wooden table, and a stool. The single window was about eight feet from the floor and six inches square. Hungry, Wilde passed the hours wondering what supper would be like —until it became clear that he wasn't going to be given any supper.

He was interrogated the following morning, and during the next week the process was to be repeated three times. On each occasion the questioning was prefaced by the senior of the six naval officers telling him that if he was sensible and answered a few simple questions he would be allowed to leave solitary confinement and join his comrades, whom he could hear exercising and skylarking in the adjoining compound. Wilde was surprised to discover that although the questioners were persistent and seemed to know a frightening amount about British submarine technicalities, there was no attempt to bully him, and no apparent annoyance at his non-committal or deliberately stupid replies.

At the end of the week he was moved to one of the compound's huts, and although he had company again, Wilde recalls this as a period of intense boredom. There were practically no games, entertainment facilities, or books, and little hope of receiving letters from England. The men were told that as the camp was only a temporary home, there was no point in putting their addresses on the severely rationed outgoing mail. Wilde stayed in the hut for four weeks, the only bright spot being the news that filtered through of the Allied invasion of Sicily.

On July 21st Wilde was on the move yet again—happily, back to Italy. With a mixed naval contingent, including other submariners from *Sahib*, he was transferred to Camp PG 52 outside La Spezia, the port between Genoa and Pisa. They arrived there on August 1st, and life was certainly more relaxed and humane than it had been in Germany. If the food was poor, at least Wilde could pass the time boxing and playing football, and with informal Italian lessons from the guards.

On September 3rd the prisoners heard that the Allies had invaded Italy; then, on September 8th, it was announced that Marshal Badoglio, the Italian Prime Minister, had signed an armistice. There was wild jubilation among both prisoners and guards. From the former's point of view, all they had to do now was sit and wait until the army came. But it was the German army that arrived in the cold grey of the next day's dawn.

They were to be entrained back to Germany, but not from La Spezia. They had to make a forty-mile march to the seaside resort of Chiavari, south of Rapallo, and catch a train from there. On the march Wilde found himself alongside Leading Seaman Davis of *Sahib*, and by the time they reached Chiavari both were agreed in one thing: they would escape from the train before it reached the Italian border.

At first prospects seemed remote. Their transport consisted of cattle trucks, and when each received its quota of thirty men the doors were slammed shut and a stout metal bar secured horizontally across the outside. Wilde and Davis managed to keep together. They squatted side by side in the dark, smelly truck, the only source of light and air being four narrow windows five feet from the floor, one in each corner of the end walls.

As his eyes grew accustomed to the gloom Wilde recognized another member of *Sahib*'s crew, Able Seaman Cheeseman. Wilde called him over and suggested he should join them in their escape. Cheeseman thought it over for a while, then decided against it. He would have loved to accompany them, but pointed out that he was the only married man of the three, was forty years old, and had three children. He felt—Wilde and Davis thought rightly—that it would be wrong to risk leaving a widow and fatherless children at this stage of the game. He reckoned he ought to accept the alternative of imprisonment in Germany. He made his decision with obvious reluctance, but assured the other two that he would do all he could to help them get away.

With much clanking of couplings, straining of hinges, and squeaking of wheels the train pulled out. Bumping and swaying on the wooden floor of the truck, Davis and Wilde debated how they could best attempt to make a break for it—if at all. The discussion grew progressively more pessimistic . . . then the train shuddered to a halt. Wilde stuck his head through one of the narrow windows and saw they were at a small village station. Immediately in front of their truck was a brake van, and a German soldier climbed down from it and began patrolling the platform. He was just passing the end of Wilde's truck for the fourth or fifth time when the train started to pull out. Rifle in hand, he jumped forward and hoisted himself to a seat on the buffers, a few feet below Wilde's window.

In his action Wilde saw their one possibility of escape. It was hazardous—but the only chance they had.

He went over to Davis and Cheeseman and told them of his plan. Wilde possessed the only coin they had. With great ceremony he tossed it—and lost. He would be the first to go.

Before leaving La Spezia Wilde had appropriated a sheet. He took it from his pack and tore it in half. Apart from being almost his only possession it would make excellent bandages should they be needed. Wilde and Davis tucked their halves inside their battledress blouses—and were ready.

Now it was up to Cheeseman. He put his head out of the window, and in excruciatingly bad German started a conversation with the soldier on the buffers. The guard replied in equally execrable English, but within a few minutes they were discussing what life would be like in Germany. As they talked Wilde made his way to one of the windows at the opposite end of the truck.

He swallowed hard, gave Davis a thumbs-up sign, and stuck his head out of the window. That much was easy. With a great deal of contorted wriggling and pulling, and suffering a crucifying pain that made him think his bones must surely crack, he freed his shoulders and arms. Now came the most dangerous moment so far: with Davis holding his feet he had to get his hips through the window and at the same time lower himself down to grab hard at the bouncing, rocking, swaying buffers below. "It couldn't have taken more than a few seconds," he says, "but it seemed an eternity. First to hold on to the buffers, then lower my feet down and under me. . . . And the train was going much faster than I'd supposed."

It was a little easier for Davis, helped from both inside the truck and outside, and soon each was straddling a buffer.

They were passing through farming country, and occasionally groups of Italians working in the fields waved to them. Wilde waved back—and it struck him as extraordinarily funny that the German guard on the buffer at the other end of the truck must have been thinking the waves were directed at him. But the grin quickly vanished as the train rounded a bend—the sun was now striking it from the side instead of behind, throwing huge shadows of himself and Davis on to the track.

Above the noise of the train he yelled at Davis, "We've got to get away from here."

Davis nodded, and suggested they should climb to the roof of the truck and crawl along it to the rear: "Like they do in the films." But Wilde shook his head and pointed out that there would almost certainly be an open platform behind the guard's van with at least one armed soldier on it. And jumping off sideways would be just as public—even if they were lucky enough to land on a soft patch of ground.

"Suddenly," says Wilde, "I was struck by the complete idiocy of the situation. There we were, riding on the buffers of a train travelling through enemy territory, with no idea of what the next move was going to be. In the truck I'd worked out how to get as far as the buffers, but no further. Finally, by a simple process of elimination, I decided there was only one direction in which we *could* go—down."

With his left hand holding hard to the coupling hook, and his right arm round the buffer, Wilde took a deep breath, curved his back, and slowly lowered himself beneath the train to within inches of the track. But the train was travelling at far too great a speed to permit him to let go his hold. The sweat poured from his face, and his muscles became a hideous nightmare of pain as he strained to maintain his grip of coupling and buffer and hold his legs away from the sleepers that flashed beneath him.

His strength—and his luck—held. Within two or three minutes the train slowed down. He let go—and was surprised at the softness of his landing.

The train did not gather speed again. It came to a halt, with Wilde hidden by one of the rear trucks. He stiffened when he heard a scraping on the gravel between the rails, then raised his head and saw Davis crawling towards him. A few seconds later came the sound of footsteps, and from between the wheels Wilde saw four pairs of jackboots crunching along the track. They came to a halt alongside where he was lying. One of the guards spat. With ironic accuracy the spittle hit Wilde in the face. Then the four pairs of jackboots continued their patrol.

Davis, however, was spotted. Wilde saw him scramble from under a truck three away from his own, but it did not appear to enter the minds of the Germans that he might have a companion. Wilde heard the five of them board the train, which started to move off almost immediately.

Wilde pushed himself as hard as he could against the ground, covering his head with his hands against the possibility of a loose coupling chain—and, sure enough, just as the last wheels thundered over him, his hands were gashed open.

But he'd done it—and in his exultation Wilde made his first mistake. Instead of waiting until the train was completely out of sight he jumped to his feet—and found himself looking into the eyes of the German guard smoking a pipe on the rear observation platform. He did not have a rifle with him, but he reached quickly for the communication cord.

His aching muscles and bleeding hands forgotten, Wilde turned his back on the train and ran.

Chapter
TWO

A Barn to Sleep in

A FEW yards from the track the ground sloped into a shallow ditch. Less than two feet deep, it offered no protection, but Wilde instinctively veered into it, still running with all the speed he could muster. A woman stepped out of the hedge, and he almost knocked her down. He was briefly aware of a gaunt face looking frightenedly at him. His mind was a turmoil, and he knew only that he must run . . . run as fast as he was able . . . get away from the train. . . .

At one point he was tempted to cross into the fields, but realized they were flat and devoid of cover. Then he saw a small white house. A few more paces and he recognized it as marking a level-crossing. As he turned towards it the level-crossing keeper came from behind a hedge: a short, stocky man in an official cap and with a woollen vest over his trousers. He moved towards Wilde, gesticulating. Almost sobbing now from a combination of pain and panic, Wilde swung a right hook that caught the Italian in the throat. Hardly slowing down, he followed this with a left to the chin that dropped the man to the ground. Wilde staggered on, wondering why there was no rifle or machine-gun fire.

The garden of the house was fenced from the track with shrubs and netting and a few strands of barbed wire. In the garden stood the crossing-keeper's wife. She had witnessed the entire drama: the train passing with one man on the buffers, another hanging under the coupling . . . the train stopping a few hundred yards from the level-crossing . . . the discovery of one of the men, the other coming towards her in a shambling run, knocking down her husband as he came.

Fortunately, this assault was more than equated by her passionate hatred of the Germans and a basic female sympathy for a defenceless man on the run. She beckoned to Wilde, opened a rickety wooden gate in the fence, and led him through her arid patch of garden to a small courtyard at the rear. He trailed after her, scattering ducks and chickens and provoking a chained dog into a frenzy of barking.

He heard a short, solitary burst of rifle fire. Wilde was not to know it, but the train had not stopped again. It had merely slowed down and passed the information of his escape to an infantry patrol that happened to be in the fields not far from the level-crossing.

Near to collapse, Wilde saw a tank of water and lurched towards it, aware of a dreadful thirst. But a warning shout from the woman stopped him. She motioned him to a clump of bushes at the back of the courtyard. Wilde tried to reach them, but his legs gave way under him. As the woman later described it to her husband, he made the bushes on all fours, *come una bestia* ("like an animal").

The woman went away. Now all Wilde wanted was to sleep. Escape . . . the train . . . the Germans . . . were all remote and meaningless. Sleep was the only thing that mattered or made sense. But the woman returned and dropped a pair of old trousers and a torn, greasy jacket on the ground beside him. She spoke to him, but, for all his Italian lessons while a prisoner, he could not understand a word she said. He could understand her gestures, however: he was to change his clothes and go.

"Looking back," says Wilde, "I don't know how I did it. I'd come to the end of the road. I was exhausted, mentally and physically. I don't think there was a muscle or bone in my body that hadn't been strained to the absolute limit. Yet somehow I managed to climb to my feet again, take off my prisoner-of-war battledress, and change into the clothes she left me. The human mind and body must have extraordinary reserves, because I was able to force myself to start walking again—out into the country beyond the house."

It was partly maize fields, partly vineyards. Wilde could see people working in the distance, and, arguing that there might be some degree of safety in numbers, he shuffled through the vineyard towards them. Then he saw three German soldiers, rifles at the ready, accompanied by an Italian policeman. They had seen him, too. There was nothing for it but a bluff. He picked up a basket lying at one end of a row of vines and moved slowly along the row, picking grapes as he went. The patrol came to the end of the row, watched him, and began talking. There was little doubt that Wilde formed the subject of their conversation, and he was certain that the clumsiness of his fingers would soon betray him.

Wilde saw one of the soldiers take a hand-grenade from his belt—the traditional German type, reminiscent of a potato-masher—and unscrew the end. To Wilde the scene was quite unreal and illusionary. He thought that perhaps he ought to run, but his feet were leaden and unresponsive. He wondered, too, why on earth the soldier needed a grenade; why not a rifle or revolver?

The patrol's conversation developed into an argument. Finally the man with the grenade seemed to brush aside the objections of his companions. His arm went back preparatory to hurling the grenade—and Wilde's legs came to life, taking him along the row of vines away from the soldiers.

There was a road alongside the vineyard, and as the grenade left the German's hand a farm lorry rattled past, sending up a thick cloud of dust. The force of the explosion knocked Wilde flat on his face, but, apart from being showered with dirt, pebbles, and leaves, he was unharmed. The dust put up by the lorry took a long time to settle, and served to hide Wilde from the patrol. His mind clearer now than at any time since leaving the train, he scrambled through to the road and made his way to the exact point at which the soldiers had been standing before they entered the vineyard.

A simple enough ruse—but it worked. The soldiers and the

policeman conferred together, and after much discussion and gesticulation left the vineyard and made for a neighbouring maize field.

Wilde began walking along the road, leaving the level-crossing behind him. He passed a number of cherry-trees—and realized he was still carrying his basket. He added some cherries to the grapes, and after about a quarter of a mile came to an uncultivated field set back from the road. In it stood a large chestnut-tree. Wilde sat behind the tree in order to be hidden from passers-by, and as he reached for the grapes he understood just why his behaviour in the vineyard had been so suspicious: instead of picking the grapes in bunches he had plucked them individually from the vine.

Before he could enjoy the joke—or the fruit—he was asleep.

He was awakened by a hand on his shoulder. Defensively he shrank back, certain the Germans had come. But the man leaning over him was a small, balding Italian of about fifty, a large smile on his wrinkled, grey-moustached face. It was morning, and Wilde guessed he must have slept for about ten hours.

The man took a bottle of wine from a haversack and said, "*Bravo ragazzo.*" This was within Wilde's vocabulary, and he found it immensely reassuring to be called a "good lad". After this conversational gambit the little man chattered away non-stop, in no way deterred by Wilde's obvious lack of comprehension. For his part, Wilde was delighted to have found a friend, and went happily and with no embarrassment when his companion led him hand in hand across the fields to his home: a small, two-storied building faced with crumbling plaster.

By the front door was a bench; sitting upon it two women. They jumped to their feet as the men approached, but when Wilde's friend called "*Sta fermo*" ("Sit still") they did. Inside the house Wilde was provided with water and a towel, and after he had washed the women came in and gave him breakfast: a large bowl of milk, bread still warm from the oven, and fruit. Then came the questions.

Despite the language barrier they managed to exchange a great deal of information. The family's name was Rovati. The man was Frederico; the younger woman was his wife, Clementina; the elder his grandmother—a remarkably youthful and sprightly ninety-seven-year-old. Wilde told his story as best he could, and in return they explained to him that he was on the outskirts of the village of Medassino, which in turn was not far from the town of Voghera, in the province of Pavia. The province was divided in two by the river Po, with Voghera and Medassino in the southern half, the Oltrepo. Being in the Po valley, the surrounding land was quite flat, but to the south were the foothills of the Emilian Apennines. Here were to be found the *partigiani* ("the partisans")—an item of information which at the time Wilde found to be only of passing interest.

During the day other members of the Rovati family arrived including Frederico's daughter, Maria. The more they talked the more Wilde was able to understand, although there were moments when he found himself quite baffled by what they were saying. At these times Maria acted as a sort of inter-preter, explaining that while Wilde was trying to speak conventional Italian the family had lapsed into the local dialect, Vogherese.

Having rested and fed, Wilde was feeling far more cheerful and optimistic. His spirits were high, and he thought that when darkness came he would make a quick dash down to the Allied lines. But when he asked how far south the Allies were Frederico replied, "*Lontano*" ("A long way"). Although his hosts had no exact idea of the extent of the Allied advance, it was clear that the front line was still at the bottom of the long Italian peninsula.

As Wilde wondered what the devil was to become of him Frederico looked at his watch and indicated that it was time to move on. Wilde felt like a helpless child being taken from one nursemaid to another, a pawn in somebody else's game—a feeling he was to experience many times in the months that followed.

It was dusk when they left the house, yet Wilde thought

that darkness somehow held more threats and dangers than the day. His fears increased when they rounded a corner and encountered a young woman sitting on a bicycle propped against a gate. Frederico, however, was undismayed, and almost nonchalantly introduced the girl, Leonina, to the *prigioniero inglese* ("the English prisoner of war"). Leonina said she would accompany them into Medassino. There were a number of houses along the highway, each with its group of people chatting on the doorstep. Frederico and Leonina exchanged greetings as they passed, but kept moving, allowing no time for a conversation to develop, Wilde was acutely aware of his vulnerability, and was sure that his very shadow shrieked his identity. He would certainly have panicked had it not been for the self-assured ease of his escorts.

He regained his courage in an odd, almost ridiculous, manner. As they entered the village proper and walked down a narrow and draughty street Wilde felt that his backside was cold. Sure enough, there was a large tear in his trousers. Says Wilde: "The fact that it must have been there all the time I was with the Rovatis, plus the fact that I had a girl walking next to me, was acutely embarrassing. For two or three minutes I wondered what to do—then realized how daft it was to worry about a triviality like that in relation to my situation as a whole."

That he was able to laugh again marked the end of Wilde's fears and pessimism. He told himself that there were going to be plenty of risks in the days ahead, but, since he had been lucky so far, why shouldn't his good fortune continue? Fortunately, too, he was a person with a capacity for closing his mind to problems and situations he preferred not to think about. He had remarkable resilience, and there was almost a jauntiness to his walk as he continued through the streets of Medassino.

They stopped for a while at Leonina's home, where his story had to be told yet again, and where the girl's mother provided him with a hot bath and a change of clothes. Then they moved on to the via Maestra and into the courtyard of a block of flats. In a corner a group of men sat round a table, drinking. Frederico introduced Wilde, and it was of considerable help that one, Pietro Goi, spoke English—with a strong American accent. He was known, in fact, as Pietro Americano, having spent about twenty years in the U.S.A. Pietro was Frederico's solution to the problem of what to do with Wilde. The sailor was English . . . Pietro spoke English —everybody's troubles were at an end! Having delivered himself of this dubious rationalization, Frederico left for home.

Pietro poured wine—and talked. He told Wilde the latest news of the War, confirming what the Rovatis had said of the impossibility of reaching the Allied lines from Medassino. He assured Wilde that he would take him to a safe hiding-place, and taught the Englishman some of his wide repertoire of Italian sign language, the most important sign from Wilde's point of view being a sharp tap with the ends of his fingers against his ribs, meaning that he was hungry. Another involved tapping the right hand against the inside of the left arm where it bent at the elbow: an injunction that the person to whom it was addressed should do something physically impossible to himself. Next came reminiscences about New York, and these were followed by a vivid description, based on the treatment handed out to captured partisans, of what would happen to anyone found aiding a British prisoner on the run—fingernails pulled out, eyes blinded, and similar pleasantries.

As the evening dragged on the men at the table left for their homes, until only one other man remained besides Wilde and Pietro. Wilde thought the talk and the drinking would continue until dawn—then Pietro's wife appeared. Reluctantly the voluble little Italian ended his chatter with the information that the safest place to sleep would be in a barn on his nephew's farm, and that the other man would take him there.

The road led back through the village and past the Rovati holding. During the entire journey his guide did not utter a word, and Wilde was grateful: he was too tired to struggle to converse in Italian. When they reached the barn Wilde climbed to the loft, slid under a pile of hay, and was soon asleep.

He awoke at dawn and sat at one of the barn's windows, watching the road and studying the pink-plastered house that lay some three hundred yards away, half hidden by trees. After about an hour a man came from the house: his escort of the previous night. He brought a chunk of bread and a steaming bowl of coffee, which he said was *caffé e latte*. Although this was self-evident, Wilde was reassured: he had begun to think the man was mute. Breakfast over, the man beckoned Wilde to follow him.

Outside the barn his companion silently handed him a cap and pointed to a long-handled spade, which Wilde obediently shouldered. They went past the farmhouse to a small, bare wooden hut at the edge of a vineyard. Wilde was told that he could stay in the hut or pretend to work between the vines—and without another word his guide walked off. Wilde's years in the Navy left him in no doubt as to which course to follow: he squatted in a corner of the hut and slept.

He must have been there for three hours when footsteps awakened him. He jumped to his feet and grabbed the spade, his only weapon in the event of his callers being the police or German soldiers. As the door opened he uttered a great sigh of relief: his visitor was a small boy of about fourteen, who greeted him with, "*Buon' giorno. Sono Dino.*"

"*Sono James*," replied Wilde.

"Ah, Gems" . . . and "Gems" was to be the way his Christian name was pronounced for the rest of his time in Italy.

Dino brought bread, hard-boiled eggs, and a bottle of wine, and Wilde reflected that at this rate there was little chance of dying of starvation. The boy stayed all that afternoon, and Wilde was pleased for the company and for the opportunity of improving his Italian. Then, at five o'clock, his taciturn escort arrived to take him back to the barn.

Next morning Pietro came to see him, and said there was no point exposing himself with daily trips to the vineyard just to sit in a hut that was less secure and comfortable than the barn. He had better stay put until a further plan had been decided upon. Wilde agreed.

Visits from Dino, sometimes accompanied by his younger brother, helped to pass the time, although Wilde was acutely embarrassed by the way the two boys hero-worshipped him: he had escaped from the Germans, and to them was something of a superman. One day no less than thirty villagers arrived *en masse* to gaze at the strange visitor in their midst.

Despite the attentions of Dino and his brother, there were still the long evenings and interminable nights. "I'd lie for hours just thinking," says Wilde. "I'd think of everything that had happened since I squeezed out of the window of the cattle truck. I'd think about Sheffield, about my parents, and about Doreen. We'd got engaged on my last leave before *Sahib* left for Malta.

"And I thought about the responsibilities I'd taken on by escaping. For one thing, I had a duty to the people who had helped me: I had to be sure none of them was victimized on my account. Of course, I had a duty to my country too—but I couldn't see at that stage what I could do about it. The Allied front was still at the foot of Italy, well south of Naples—about four hundred miles from Medassino. There were no longer any illusions in my mind about the armistice meaning an immediate occupation of Italy. And by no stretch of the imagination could I see myself covering four hundred miles of enemy-occupied territory without being caught on the way.

"On the other hand I reckoned I couldn't just sit in the barn—or wherever else they decided to shift me to—and wait for the War to end. I'd think vaguely of joining the partisans, but I didn't know where to find them—nor, it appeared, did anybody else. Another thing: my Italian, although good enough for amusing conversations with Dino, was still pretty primitive. And there was something else, too. It's funny how deep-rooted service tradition can become; for even as a prisoner of war on the run I still was dominated by the age-old maxim: never volunteer!

"I thought a lot about the Navy, too. You see, it's easy enough to face danger in the fore end of a submarine: all the thinking and decision-taking is done by the skipper in the control-room. But being on my own and having to make my own decisions gave danger an added dimension.

"Frankly I'd never been interested in shouldering that sort of responsibility. I had no ambition to be even a Leading Seaman, far less a Petty Officer. And as long as I was in naval surroundings that philosophy worked admirably for me and for thousands of other A.B.s. But now I *had* to make decisions; I *had* to shoulder responsibilities—whether I liked it or not. I could only hope that my decisions would be the right ones and that I wouldn't let anyone down.

"And as the first step towards doing anything—anything at all—I decided that I'd have to master Italian until I could speak it with the fluency of a native."

Chapter
THREE

The Via Sant' Ambrogio

ON the fifth day of his stay in the barn a man giving Pietro Americano's name by way of identification escorted Wilde from the farm to the home of Egidio Ferretti, on the main Medassino road. "This move marked the beginning of a strange and curiously distinct period," says Wilde. "It was to last a long time. Yet, looking back, I don't recall it so much as a complete picture, but rather as a series of snapshots—a jumbled pattern of isolated incidents."

He stayed in Ferretti's handsome *palazzo* for five days. Once, while he was asleep, the Germans came asking about an escaped prisoner of war. His host's denial was convincing in that the soldiers did not make a search of the building, but they were persistent in their belief that the man who had jumped from the train ten days earlier was still in the area. Ferretti said it would be dangerous to stay in Medassino for a while, and on bicycles they made for the mountains of the Emilian Apennines. There, in the village of Castello, Wilde stayed with a Signora Maria—an old lady who was told that he was an Italian submariner struck deaf and dumb in an English depth-charge attack and who had deserted rather than face hospital life under the Germans.

After three weeks of silence and boredom, another move. Escorted by a man called Vittorio Morini, Wilde went down to the plains again, this time into the town of Voghera itself, to stay in the flat of Vittorio's sister, Teresa Berti, and her husband, Giuseppe. It was argued that Voghera, the largest town in the Oltrepo, with a population of several thousands, offered a greater degree of concealment than a small village, where every new face was an occasion for excitement and gossip.

Wilde's host was a tiny man in his forties, a mechanic with a local transport firm. He was as quiet as his wife was talkative, and it was thanks to her that by the time Wilde's stay with the Bertis came to an end he was speaking Italian like a native, even to the extent of a convincing vocabulary of Vogherese dialect. He was still known as Gems, although in terms of his future movements Teresa and Giuseppe decided it would be safer if he could become accustomed to calling himself by the Italian equivalent of James: Giacomo.

At first, however, on walks around the town, Wilde maintained an absolute silence, and was introduced to friends of the Bertis as a nephew from Rome struck dumb after a throat accident. "I was certainly apprehensive about going into the streets during those early days," Wilde recalls, "but my misgivings soon lost out to the effect of the boredom of being confined in a small flat. And if I did nothing to draw attention to myself I wasn't too exposed. The town was run by the German army and the Italian Brigata Nera. These—and Fascist civilians—were the people I had to take care to avoid, for, despite the armistice and the sympathies of the majority of the population, Voghera was part of a German-occupied country, very much at war with the Allies."

Life outside the flat was always hazardous, and not without moments of acute peril. There was a shortage of food in the town, and Wilde and Giuseppe would cycle in the evenings towards Medassino to see what they could 'find' in the fields. One expedition took them along a road under a railway bridge. This was classified as a military objective, and was guarded by Italian soldiers. Wilde was some fifty yards ahead of Giuseppe, and, to his consternation, a sentry ordered him to stop. Wilde dismounted and listened in silence to the demand for his papers. Nervously he waited for Giuseppe to come and tell his Italian submariner story. But his friend's thought processes were quicker than Wilde's: a former rating in the Italian navy would still need the regulation two identity cards, one Italian and one German. As he displayed his own cards Giuseppe told the sentry that his nephew was mentally deficient. Wilde immediately adopted what he hoped was a suitably lunatic facial expression—which nearly dissolved into a sigh of relief when the sentry accepted Giuseppe's explanation as being a good enough reason for not having an identity card. They rode on.

As Wilde's Italian improved, his feeling of boredom increased. "I'd help with the housework and read Italian papers and books, and took to going for walks and cycle rides by myself.

"One day some desire for a bit of fun made me take the road to the level-crossing where I'd escaped from the train. It was all a bit of a lark—until an armed Italian sentry came from the crossing-keeper's house. He ordered me to stop and asked for my papers.

"This was undoubtedly my worst moment yet. It really did seem as though the game was up. For although the soldier was bespectacled and frail-looking, he had a rifle. I took a chance and said, 'I don't have my papers with me. Anyway, you don't really want to see them. I'm only going to Medassino. Let me through this time and I'll be sure to remember them in future.' I gave him a big smile—which was a great effort—and he waved me on with an admonition to abide by regulations.

"But the encounter, although frightening, had one great significance: it meant my Italian had passed its first big test."

Wilde acknowledges that while these episodes are amusing in retrospect, at the time they were fraught with danger—such as the incident of the football match. . . .

On one of his rides Wilde passed a group of German soldiers playing football on the outskirts of Medassino. A misdirected kick sent the ball into the road in front of him. He swerved to avoid it, lost his balance, and fell to the ground. Three of the soldiers walked across, laughing, and examined him for injuries. One said in bad Italian that as they were a player short he could keep goal. Impulsively he accepted, and subsequent doubts about the wisdom of his action were forgotten as he became totally absorbed in the game—so much so, indeed, that he was quite disappointed when a lorry arrived to take the soldiers back to barracks. The captain of his side put an arm round his shoulders and thanked him for playing. As Wilde rode back to Voghera the thought came to him that one of his team-mates might well have been the soldier who had lobbed a hand-grenade at him.

The weeks became months, and Wilde grew to accept his curious life in Voghera. December came, and by now the Fifth Army had crossed the Volturno, while the Eighth had reached the Sangro, ninety miles north of Foggia. But the advance was slow, and the Allied front line still many miles to the south.

One evening Wilde felt particularly restless and decided to go for a walk, even though it was approaching the nine o'clock curfew. He strolled aimlessly, and soon had no clear idea in which part of the town he was. The streets were deserted, and he enjoyed the solitude. Consequently he was a little annoyed when two men came towards him along the street. Anxious to keep as far from other people as possible, he crossed to the other pavement. The two men also crossed. Wilde sensed danger.

His moodiness gone, his brain alert, he crossed back. So did the two men. Wilde stopped, made certain there was a wall squarely behind his back, and waited. Except for the opaque light from a half-clouded moon, the street was dark.

"*Scusami, che Lei ha un' sigaretta, per favore?*" ("Excuse me, do you have a cigarette, please?") asked the smaller of the two men. He was a little taller than Wilde, with a distinctive, foxy face decorated with a small Hitler-like moustache, and was aged about thirty-five. His companion was younger, tall, and heavily built. He was standing behind the other man.

"*Mi dispiace, ma non la ho*" ("I'm sorry, but I haven't one"), Wilde replied. At this the big man stepped forward, pulled Wilde towards him by the collar of his coat, and hit him hard and quickly in the middle of the face. Wilde felt as though his nose had run into a brick wall, and was conscious of blood spurting down and sprinkling his clothes. He swore, surprised as well as angry, and lashed out at the man. His fist landed squarely where he himself had been hit. He felt a moment's satisfaction, and then, as his mind cleared, realized he had struck out in near-panic. If he was to take on the two men successfully he knew he would need a cool head.

He hit the smaller man in the solar plexus, and followed this with a kick low in the stomach. The man fell and lay still.

As the big man moved in again, Wilde hit him flush in the mouth, but he seemed to be no more deterred than an elephant would have been. His full weight seemed to come upon Wilde, and the two men fell to the ground. A massive knee was in Wilde's chest, and he saw two immense hands coming for his throat. Somehow he managed to wriggle free, but as he staggered to his feet he could not avoid his adversary's powerful shoulder, which, rising from under him, caught him in the base of the lungs and banged him hard against the wall. His body was completely without breath, and his head spun after its collision with the brickwork.

Again the big man came at him. Instinctively Wilde pushed out a left. It was ignored rather than parried. A blow under one eye knocked Wilde down again. He was scarcely back on his feet before another blow sent him staggering down once more. For some reason the big man did not immediately dive on Wilde, and he was able to draw one agonized breath before rising on jellied legs. Again the big man advanced, and Wilde was forced to fight on the retreat. This tactic met with a little more success, for while he had to sustain two glancing, but painful, blows to the face, he was able, in return, to close one of his opponent's eyes and split his upper lip.

Wilde thought quickly. . . . He stopped, lowered his hands as though exhausted, and waited. "Sure enough," he recalls, "the big fellow moved in for the kill—and signalled it by opening his tremendous shoulders. At the last second I ducked and slid under his fist. I slipped quickly to the right, collecting every ounce of my remaining strength, and concentrated it into a blow under his left ear.

"It was at this moment that the smaller man climbed to his feet and took advantage of the fact that my back was no longer protected by the wall. Fortunately, however, his companion had buckled at the knees—and some instinct warned me to swing round. My first blow—automatic rather than scientific—hit him hard on the point of his chin. He fell down for a second time.

"I had time to draw two quick breaths, then heard the big man, who was stumbling off into the shadows, call to his friend. They'd had enough. Far from being elated, I felt somehow disappointed at not having a more positive victory. I ran after the big man, caught him by his coat, and swung him round. Too close for a proper knock-out blow, I drew my elbow back to my side and gave vent to all my fury and bad temper with a massive punch to his Adam's apple. He gave a sort of gurgling sob and crumpled to the ground. Before he reached it I helped him on his way with a kick in the groin.

"The smaller man was now well away down the street. The fight—absolutely pointless, unless the motive had been robbery, or was a case of mistaken identity—was over."

Wilde limped from the street to find he was near the via Sant' Ambrogio, where the Bertis lived. He hurried home, hoping to sneak quietly to bed, but Giuseppe was waiting for him and soon had the outline of the story. Thinking he recognized the smaller man from Wilde's description, he went out. When he returned a few minutes later he was smiling. He had seen the men standing dejectedly at a near-by corner, and assured Wilde he would know where to find the smaller man.

Wilde thought no more of Giuseppe's remarks. He was content to bathe his wounds and sleep. But the following evening his eyes nearly popped from their head when his smiling but dishevelled host came home, his knuckles bruised and swollen. Sheepishly he explained that he had found the smaller man and had given him what he'd been asking for.

At Christmas Wilde felt acutely miserable at being away from home on this particularly family festival. Teresa described him as being *nervoso*—a common condition in Italy, she assured him. Knowing consumer goods were scarce, and that neither the Morinis nor the Bertis were wealthy, Wilde did not expect any presents—but they gave him a splendid new pair of shoes, two pairs of socks, and a handsome double-breasted suit. He realized the shoes must have cost the equivalent of £12 on the black market, and dared not contemplate the price of the suit. He was overwhelmed: the two had surely done enough in risking their lives hiding him without the need for gifts bought at great financial sacrifice; while he could offer them nothing in return except his thanks.

Although it seems unreal to him now, Wilde did not think it odd at the time when, after two and a half months with the Bertis, the Morinis suggested he should take a holiday at their little farm at Medassino. Wilde accepted—but became aware quickly that the relative safety of populous Voghera was absent in the village. His fears increased when he bumped into Pietro Goi. In an excited flow of English and Italian he asked where Wilde had been staying. Instinctively Wilde did not mention either the Morinis or the Bertis, but said he was living in the mountains and was just on a cycle ride. He refused Pietro's invitation to dinner, and, to complete the deception, headed out of Medassino towards the mountains before making a detour back to the farm.

"I don't know why I lied to Pietro," says Wilde, "or turned down his offer of a meal. It was automatic, inspired by caution rather than doubt, since he had certainly proved to be a friend and protector in the early days. Maybe it was my overall uneasiness and sense of insecurity at being away from Voghera. I wasn't sorry at the end of seven days to cycle back to the Bertis' flat in the via Sant' Ambrogio."

It was perhaps as well that Wilde was not fully aware of the delicate balance between freedom and discovery. It was certainly a good thing that his friends were ever mindful of his danger. One day Clementina Rovati, wife of his first host in Medassino, saw him wandering among the stalls in the Voghera market. Her first thought was to approach him and learn what had happened to him in the months since they had last met. Then she remembered the gossip in Medassino: rumours that the Rovatis had harboured an escaped British prisoner. It was not impossible for someone to see her talking to a stranger, guess the truth, and hurry to the Brigata Nera headquarters in the via Cavour. Clementina suppressed her goodwill and curiosity and walked away.

One of Wilde's voluntary duties was to look after the few hens Giuseppe kept in the courtyard at the back of the house. With them were some hens owned by the woman in a flat upstairs. The wife of a civil servant permanently away in Germany, she was known to be strongly anti-British. Wilde was in the yard one day when the woman called from her balcony, "Giacomo, would you please let my hens out, and see if there are any eggs for me?"

Wilde did so and shouted back, "Yes, there are quite a few."

Then, to his horror, Wilde realized that he had replied in English.

The woman on the balcony called, "Goodness, he speaks English," and disappeared indoors. Wilde went to Teresa's kitchen and found her trembling with terror. He told her not to worry: he would leave immediately, so that at least the Bertis would not be caught red-handed when the Germans came. With essentially feminine reasoning Teresa said he must stay: it was his duty to protect her. Fortunately, the Germans did not come either that day or the next, and their fears diminished. It appeared that if their neighbour was surprised that the nephew from Rome could speak English, she did not think there was anything sinister about it.

He had a far more dangerous experience one Friday morning in the piazza Duomo. He was leaning on his bicycle watching the market-day scene when he became aware that someone to his left was staring at him. He turned as casually as he could and found himself looking into the astonished face of the woman he had nearly knocked over when he escaped from the train. It was all he could do to keep hold of his machine, although he experienced no impulse to run: for a full ten seconds he was too paralysed with shock to move a finger. As his body relaxed he still did not move away, but merely turned his head and watched the woman's reflection in the window of a shop bordering the piazza. But his attempt at calm indifference was of no avail: after a few seconds of puzzled hesitation she made towards a group of Brigata Nera standing at the far side of the square. Now Wilde did not hesitate: he jumped on to his bicycle, headed down the nearest alleyway, and was back in the Bertis' flat within the minute.

Not long afterwards Teresa came in. With almost theatrical drama the first thing she did was to fall on her knees and offer up a prayer. Then she explained: she had known Wilde was going to the market, and it was now cordoned off by *fascisti*. All the men there were having to show their papers, and Teresa had been certain Wilde was among them.

The danger had not yet passed. Next morning—Wilde wondered at their inefficiency in waiting so long—the Italian authorities began a house-to-house search of the town. The Bertis learned that all streets were to be barricaded off and searched, but in no specific order, so as to introduce an element of surprise.

The Bertis evolved a plan for concealing Wilde when the via Sant' Ambrogio's turn came. Giuseppe and Wilde removed a dozen tiles from the kitchen floor, and eight hours of digging, the earth surreptitiously emptied at the back of the courtyard, produced a hole large enough for Wilde to climb into without too much discomfort. The tiles were cemented to a board resting on four wooden props set into the floor of the hole. From above the hiding-place was invisible, and, after the arduous non-stop effort that had created it, it came almost as an anticlimax when the search was called off after two days with only half the town covered. Gossip had it that the search had revealed a number of illegal food hoards, some of them in the homes of embarrassingly senior citizens.

Says Wilde: "The search of the town brought into sharp focus the pointlessness of the life I was leading. I was achieving nothing—except exposing the Bertis to unnecessary dangers. But the Allied line was still half a country away—in March it was on the front from Anzio to Monte Cassino—and the partisans seemed mythological improbabilities as far as Voghera was concerned. Yet I owed it to myself, my country, and the Bertis to do something positive. I couldn't spend the rest of the War waiting to jump into a hole under the kitchen floor. What I needed was some sign, some guidance."

On March 31st Wilde celebrated his twenty-fourth birthday, and Giuseppe presented him with a quarter-pound packet of English tea, of what age and from what source Wilde dared not inquire. April 24th marked the anniversary of the loss of *Sahib*, and on June 1st, 1944, he set in motion the events that were to lead to the sign and guidance for which he had been waiting—although they did not come in the form he had expected. . . .

On that day Wilde rode into Medassino, and on a whim cycled to the farm of Pietro Americano's nephew to take a look at the barn which had been his first real hiding-place.

Coincidentally Pietro and his wife had been visiting the farm, and were just leaving as Wilde cycled past. Wilde stopped, and they chatted inconsequentially about the "old days" of the previous September. With Pietro were two young girls aged about seventeen and fifteen, whom Wilde had met briefly when escorted from the barn of Pietros nephew to the little hut in the vineyard. They greeted him warmly, and when there was a lull in Pietro's compulsive chatter the elder girl took up the conversation. Where had he been? What had he been doing? Where was he staying? Who had been hiding him all these months? Wilde's replies were evasive, but the girl was undeterred.

Wasn't he lonely? Wouldn't he like a girl friend to take to the pictures? Couldn't they meet again soon? The direction the questions were taking was not only embarrassing, but dangerous. Pietro's wife looked annoyed, but said nothing. Pietro smiled shyly, but said nothing. Wilde thought carefully, realizing the folly of bluntly snubbing the girl, and replied tactfully that he indeed hoped they would meet again soon. Before the conversation could develop further he mounted his bicycle and rode away.

As he cycled back to Voghera he wondered if he had offended the girl: that out of spite she would report his presence to the Fascists. It did not occur to him that the real danger would spring from not having discouraged overtures of friendship sufficiently.

And that is what happened. The girl went from friend to

friend, saying she was as good as engaged to an Englishman. On occasions she omitted "as good as". Inevitably she told one person who told another, who told another . . . who told the *fascisti*. A search-party arrived at her father's farm.

At first the girl denied all knowledge of any British prisoner of war. Little attention was paid to her, for it was thought that Wilde was hiding somewhere in the farmhouse or its out-buildings. The house was almost stripped Doors were wantonly knocked in . . . rifle butts crashed through lath-and-plaster partitions . . . bayonets poked and slashed indiscriminately where a man might be concealed. Finally, after much irreparable damage had been done, the young Italian captain in charge of the search-party accepted there was no man hiding there.

Attention returned to the girl. Understandably perhaps, it needed few threats of arrest and imprisonment for her to break down. Sobbing, she gave the name of Pietro Americano.

It was now evening. Warning her and her family not to attempt to leave the house, and posting two sentries to make certain they obeyed, the captain left. Early next morning he was banging at the door of Pietro's flat in the via Maestra.

It was June 10th, 1944. Pietro was dragged to the courtyard, where a police van was waiting to drive him to the Brigata Nera building in the via Cavour. Neighbours attempted to comfort his screaming wife . . . and Medassino was in ferment.

By a fortunate chance Vittorio Morini's sister Giuseppina was passing the Goi home when the police van left. Realizing the danger, she cycled to Voghera. Wilde was the only person at home—cleaning the kitchen stove—when the front door burst open and the panic-stricken Giuseppina staggered in. "Escape, escape," she panted. "Pietro has been arrested. He's bound to know where you are living, and if he doesn't tell them he'll be sent to Germany. Escape now, while you can."

Wilde was just beginning to succeed in calming her down when Teresa returned. The little woman showed no sign of anxiety for her husband or herself. Instead she said that Wilde was to dress in his best clothes and she would take him to the home of a friend, Serafina, where he would be safe. As for herself and Giuseppe, she (like Wilde) did not believe Pietro knew of the link between them. Anyway, his going to Serafina's would give them time to think. Giuseppina was to return to Medassino and forget that she had ever come to Voghera.

Serafina's mother was unhappy at first at the idea of harbouring an escaped prisoner whose capture was the main concern of every Fascist official in the town; but her natural warm-heartedness won through.

In the middle of the afternoon Serafina's married sister, Maria, arrived with news of the day's events. She had met one of her husband's friends, a Fascist officer, who had told her they were all looking for a Captain Jim, an English spy operating from Voghera.

He had also told her that Pietro Americano was not to be sent to Germany: he was to be shot immediately.

Serafina and her mother gasped at this announcement. For Wilde the immediate emotion was of relief: relief that inaction and indecision were now over. With a polite *a rivederci* he walked from the flat and returned to the via Sant' Ambrogio.

When he announced that he was going to give himself up there was at first incredulity, then protests and arguments. Finally, when Teresa and Giuseppe understood that he was adamant, tears. There was much hand-shaking and kissing and oaths of eternal friendship. There were strict instructions —which rather ignored the need to keep his Voghera contacts secret—to write to them from prison. They exchanged plans to visit each other when the War was over. After a quick rehearsal of the story he would tell of his nine months of freedom Wilde hurried from the flat towards the piazza Duomo and the via Cavour.

"I did not trust myself to look back," says Wilde. "And as I walked I found myself praying for the safety of those two wonderful people. My praying was so intense that before I had time to analyse my own actions and predicament I had reached the limestone façade of the Brigata Nera building."

Chapter
FOUR

Colonel Fiorentini

AT this moment Wilde's great strength was his remarkable ability to close his mind when he wished to any thoughts of cause or effect: his capacity—born of long training and discipline—for treating an action as something complete in itself. Consequently the act of surrender was almost a conditioned reflex, something that had to be done. The question of attendant or implied hazards would come later.

As he passed under the archway of the barracks Wilde said "*Buona sera*" to the sentry, who grunted a "*Buona sera*" in reply, but made no attempt to stop him.

Inside the central courtyard Wilde found himself facing a stone wall on which was painted: *Credere, Ubbidire, Combattere* ("Believe, Obey, Fight"). Under the words the wall was spattered with a honeycomb of small holes, the greatest concentration of them about four feet from the ground. As he approached Wilde thought they looked like bullet-holes. The wall was, in fact, the execution site for political prisoners.

To his left Wilde could see two open doors leading to the cookhouse and a lavatory. On the floor above was a balcony rail; behind it were the doors of what he guessed to be sleeping quarters and offices. To his right were three heavily barred doors, which he assumed were the cells. He was still regarding the scene when a tall corporal came up and asked what he wanted. "*Comandante*," said Wilde. The corporal directed him up a flight of stairs leading to the balcony. At the top Wilde found a door labelled "Colonnello Fiorentini."

"That name in itself was enough to make me realize at last what I'd let myself in for," says Wilde. "I'd heard of Fiorentini. He was the man, far more villainous than the Germans, who had terrorized the Oltrepo during the past fifteen months. I remembered both Pietro and Ferretti telling me dreadful stories of torn-off fingernails, nostrils plugged with lighted cigarettes, and similar tortures. But it was too late to think of turning back. I rang the bell at the side of the door."

It was opened by a dapper little man dressed in civilian clothes. From his age Wilde knew he could not be Fiorentini, but gathered from his manner that he was some sort of officer. "What can I do for you?" he asked.

"I believe you are looking for an Englishman," Wilde replied in Italian.

"Yes, we are."

"Well . . . I'm the man you're looking for."

The effect was extraordinary—as though a gun had gone off just behind the little man's head. He gave a startled jump, went red in the face, and stamped his foot furiously on the floor. "You are a stupid liar," he yelled. "What do you . . . ?" His voice trailed off, his eyes narrowed, then he said in a whisper, "Speak to me in English."

Wilde smiled. "I am the man the Fascists have been looking for," he said in broad Yorkshire.

At this the man came noisily to life. "Duty guard!" he shouted. "Sergeant-Major! Sergeant! At the double!"

In a moment the small office was packed with soldiers waving revolvers and brandishing rifles with fixed bayonets.

"But the worst part of it," says Wilde, "was the almost uncontrollable excitement. It needed only one small spark for them to have filled me with bullets. I was terrified. Then the young colonel—as his rank turned out to be—ordered them to port arms, and I knew the moment of danger had passed."

The colonel dismissed all but two of the soldiers, had Wilde searched, then allowed him to sit, leaving the guards standing by the door. He was about to sit himself when the two soldiers stiffened to attention. As Wilde turned to see the newcomer the colonel said, "Ah, Pastorelli. Please come in"—and Wilde felt sick in the stomach.

For if Fiorentini, a colonel in the regular army, was hated and feared, but respected, Pastorelli was hated and feared, but despised. A former member of the now non-existent OVRA, the Italian equivalent of the Gestapo, he was an agent of the *Sicherheitspolizei*, the German Security Police.

"Again stories flashed through my mind," says Wilde. "Ten young Vogheresi shot one morning for not giving information. Three men and a woman burned in their farmhouse on suspicion of having harboured a partisan. And of a boasted rivalry in techniques tried out by Pastorelli and his German colleagues in the via Scarabelli. And also Pastorelli's nickname: *la iena di Fiorentini* ('Fiorentini's hyena')."

Wilde saw the face of a man in his middle thirties, pale to the point of bloodlessness, with a hooked and pendulous nose and a receding forehead accentuated by a retreating hairline. His lips were small and thin, and his pale blue eyes were sunk deep behind steel-rimmed glasses. The unhealthy whiteness of his face was heightened by his clothing. Above what appeared to be dark grey civilian trousers he wore a black shirt and tie and a black leather belt. Around his left wrist he had a Security Police brassard, but no other marks of rank.

He spoke quietly in halting English. "I am Pastorelli. Stand up. I have lived in England and hate your country. I shall do all I can to make life uncomfortable for you. Now we will talk in Italian for the benefit of the colonel. Sit down."

Wilde wondered what the curious little man would do to Teresa and Giuseppe if ever they fell into his hands.

The colonel pointed to busts of Hitler and Mussolini on his desk and asked, "Do you know who they are?"

Without stopping to think, Wilde replied, "Yes, a pair of comical apes." Immediately he received a vicious blow across the mouth from the back of Pastorelli's hand. He was astonished at the strength the slightly built little man could muster. As he sucked at his swelling lips he could feel the blood trickling down from the corner of his mouth.

Then came the questions, some shouted, others whispered; some from the colonel, others from Pastorelli, who stood out of sight behind Wilde's left shoulder.

"How do you come to be so well dressed?"

"Various people have been kind to me."

"How do you speak Italian so fluently?"

"I've been in hiding a long time."

"Where?"

"Lots of different places."

"How did you know we were looking for an Englishman?"

"Lots of people have been talking about it in the area."

Wilde began to feel that the interrogation was easier than he had thought it would be. They seemed prepared to accept his answers without qualification. And his technique of taking his time and thinking carefully before replying seemed sound. But the pace quickened. The questions were repeated in slightly different forms. "We want exact answers, do you understand?" said Pastorelli.

After this warning, a vague answer earned him a jolting blow under the base of the skull from the ball of Pastorelli's hand. Soon his head was aching, and he found it increasingly difficult to concentrate on his cover story. As well as replying accurately he was encouraged to answer speedily, the difference being that a slow answer resulted in a chop across the side of his face with the edge of Pastorelli's right hand. The interrogation dissolved into a sequence of question . . . delay . . . blow to the side of the face . . . vague answer . . . blow to the base of the skull . . . more precise answer.

"Although my brain was getting scrambled," says Wilde, "I appreciated that the most sensible thing was to half-answer innocuous questions quickly and concentrate on not giving any information that could incriminate my friends. This meant not speaking in the strong Vogherese accent that was now almost second nature to me: it would have been the surest way of telling Pastorelli where I'd spent the past eight months. It was bad enough just to be interrogated in a foreign language, without having to worry about the accent

I used—as well as having to reply quickly to avoid Pastorelli's fists."

And so it went on.

"Where did you shave today?"

"In a stream just out of town. Near Medassino."

"Where have you been hiding?"

"In the mountains."

"Which mountains?"

"I don't know the names of your mountains. But these were about fifteen miles south of Godiasco." Wilde knew that in this region partisan bands were thought to be operating.

"Where did you get your civilian clothing?"

"From somebody in La Spezia in exchange for a Red Cross parcel when I was a prisoner. That was last September."

"And your Italian money?"

"I worked in the mountains for it, cleaning out stables and cowsheds."

"How do you come to speak Italian so well?"

"I was taught at school in England and took lessons from the guards in camp."

"How did you know where to come to surrender?"

"I've often been to Voghera and know the town quite well."

"Why did you decide to surrender?"

"I was passing through Medassino this morning and saw a commotion in one of the streets. A man called Pietro was being dragged from his home. I was told the man was accused of hiding an Englishman called Jim. My name is Jim, so I thought it only proper to give myself up and clear an innocent man."

"Do you know the man you saw being arrested?"

"I think I remember him giving me some bread in the early days, but I can't be sure."

"Would you recognize him if he was brought in front of you?"

Wilde could only reply: "I don't know. Why not try?"

Pastorelli and the colonel whispered together by the door, then sent a guard to fetch Pietro. Wilde was told to stand by the window. It was not many minutes before Pietro was half thrown into the room. He had a black eye and a cut lip. His nose had been bleeding, and his face and neck were sprinkled with congealed blood. He seemed deathly frightened and on the verge of collapse. But he found a reserve of courage, and managed to stand erect and still in front of his friend. Wilde knew he must act quickly

"Why, yes," he said, surprise in his voice, "I do remember this man. He was the one who gave me the bread all those months ago. But he had no idea I was an Englishman In those days I didn't trust anyone."

Pastorelli had missed a vital trick in letting him speak first. Now Wilde had given Pietro a lead and could only pray he would take advantage of it.

Pietro was asked if what Wilde said was true. He gave a description of his meeting with Wilde in Medassino which, by good fortune, tallied with Wilde's. Cold-eyed, Pastorelli fired a rapid succession of questions. "Are you telling me the whole truth? . . . Do you know the penalty for lying? . . . Are you sure you have never seen this Englishman on any other occasion? . . ." And so on.

To Wilde Pietro appeared an uneasy and unconvincing witness as he stood with his head on his chest and shuffling his feet while he gave whispered answers to Pastorelli's questions. But after his final reply Pastorelli stared at him, first from one angle then another, exchanged nods with the colonel, and told the guards to take Pietro out.

"You can go home," said the colonel. Wilde looked away in case Pietro should try to catch his eye. Seconds later he heard a tap running in the courtyard, and guessed that Pietro would be trying to clean himself up before returning home to his wife, Adele. His immediate feeling was one of relief that his friend had not suffered too severely on his account—then he remembered that Pietro was a compulsive chatterbox, and hoped the Italian would have sense enough to keep silent for once. Pastorelli was certain to have all gossip from the village reported back to him now. Then came the self-recrimination: a return of that overwhelming sense of guilt at the way in which he had exposed innocent people to such grave hazards.

The colonel—Wilde had heard one of the soldiers address him as Colonel Passerini—asked Wilde if he had eaten that day.

"I haven't had a proper meal for a long time," said Wilde. "Only grapes and other fruit and an occasional loaf of bread."

"Rubbish. You're the picture of health. You couldn't look so well on just fruit and bread."

Wilde shrugged. "It's the truth."

Perhaps Pastorelli was bored. Whatever the reason, he told Passerini, "Send him below for some food."

The guards escorted him to the cookhouse, handed him over to a fat and dirty cook, and retired to the courtyard. The cook was assisted by his wife, who babbled sympathetically: "Poor lad. What a shame. Poor child."

The thick bean soup and slice of black bread and jam were almost inedible after the relatively splendid meals on which he had been living, but he forced it all down to give some substance to his bread-and-grapes story. As soon as he had finished he was escorted to the cells.

The one in which Wilde was locked was dark, dirty, and depressing. On one wall was a broad plank of wood furnished with a bale of stinking straw and two torn blankets. Wilde took off his jacket, folded it into a pillow, threw the straw into a corner, and lay on the bare bunk between the blankets.

"God knows I was tired," says Wilde, "and stiff and aching from the blows I'd received. But I couldn't sleep. Doubts, fears, self-reproach, came in a confused rush. What had I done? I'd thrown away my liberty, but I had no guarantee that I'd succeeded in safeguarding the Bertis. On the other hand Pietro would not now be shot. What would happen to me next? Would I be sent to Germany or executed there and then in Voghera? The thoughts crowded and nagged."

After about half an hour the door of the cell was flung open and a man thrown in. He picked himself up, violently cursing all Fascists and Germans. It took him some four or five minutes to calm down—and then saw Wilde for the first time. Who was he, and what was he doing? When Wilde replied that he was an escaped English prisoner the man did not seem particularly surprised, and his general attitude was far too naïve to be true. Wilde's suspicions were confirmed when the man began asking questions about the people with whom Wilde had been hiding in Voghera. By way of reply Wilde went to the door and shouted for the guard. When he came Wilde told him that if they wanted to send in a spy they should at least select an intelligent one. Without a word his 'fellow-prisoner' was removed from the cell.

Again he tried to sleep, but sleep still eluded him. He paced his cell, thinking of home and the Navy, his family and the Bertis, and—most of all—of death and how he would face it.

He walked up and down for some time before he saw in the half-darkness a vague shape under his bunk: a heavy pole and two bricks which had been left there for some reason—or, more probably, for no reason. It did not take long to appreciate the practical possibilities of these items. He placed one brick on top of the other close to the door. Using them as a fulcrum, he wedged the pole under the door and levered it upward off its pins. But the lever worked more easily than he had expected, and the door fell outward into the courtyard with a deafening crash. Wilde dropped the pole and dived under the blankets, feigning sleep. Understandably the guard was not deceived. He swore and shouted at Wilde, made him lift the door back into position, then walk backward into his cell with his hands above his head. Before he locked the door he drove the butt of his rifle hard into Wilde's groin. The pain remained for the rest of the night, and all efforts at sleep were abandoned.

Morning came with the bells of the Duomo announcing early Mass. Wilde was escorted to the lavatory, then to the tap in the courtyard for a quick wash, but his request for breakfast was received with contemptuous laughter. He was, however, permitted to stay in the sunshine of the courtyard instead of returning to his cell.

As he sat by the railings that bordered the via Cavour he saw a woman staring at him from the opposite side of the street: Teresa. She was standing quite rigid, her expression anguished and tense, and Wilde was appalled at the risk she was running. He felt certain that the sentry would notice her odd behaviour, and so he climbed to his feet and hurried to a corner of the courtyard that was hidden from the street.

The morning dragged on until, at nine-thirty, a sergeant and two privates marched him to the office where he had been questioned the previous evening. This time neither Passerini nor Pastorelli was present. Instead, seated behind the desk was a tall, white-haired old man in officer's uniform. The sergeant addressed him as *colonnello*, and Wilde knew he had finally met Fiorentini. He stood to attention, aware of the thumping of his heart, and determined not to make any supposedly witty remarks.

For half an hour he was asked much the same questions as he had answered the night before—and gave the same answers. Fiorentini gave no sign of believing or disbelieving him. When the interrogation was over the colonel said to the sergeant, "This man will work. He can start by cleaning this floor."

"Sir, I am very hungry. Can I have something to eat first?"

Fiorentini's face purpled—literally. "Who the devil do you think you are? How dare you tell me you need food? You are here in civilian clothing, which means I can have you shot as a spy. Shot. Now. Without trial. Without delay . . . Get to work and be thankful you are still alive."

So he scrubbed the office and was then locked in his cell.

Later in the day he heard lorries drive into the courtyard, and there was a confused babel of shouts, screams, and curses. He learned later that eighteen prisoners had been brought to the barracks; nine men and nine women. They were parents of local partisans. First locked in the cell adjoining Wilde's, they were then taken into the courtyard, a pair at a time. The man was stripped to the waist and whipped with a cat-o'-nine-tails while his wife was forced to watch. The screams were a sound more terrible than anything Wilde had ever heard. When the ninth whipping was over the prisoners were bundled into the lorries and driven away. He never discovered what became of them.

His only meal that day was a mug of coffee and a slice of

bread, and when he fell asleep it was from sheer exhaustion. He was awakened the following morning by the guard banging at the door. "Someone to see you," he said as he fumbled with the lock. Wilde's heart sank: he was positive he was to be taken to the courtyard to see Teresa and Giuseppe. Instead an attractive girl in Fascist uniform entered the cell and was locked in with him.

She smiled. "I hope you don't mind me visiting you, but I was curious to see what an Englishman looked like. I persuaded them to let me slip in without the authorities knowing." She sat on the bunk beside Wilde and spoke of how hard it was being on one's own in a strange country . . . of her preference for men who went away to fight instead of staying behind at H.Q. . . ."

She seemed a nice enough girl; and attractive, with her lively eyes and warm, feminine smell. Wilde was certainly not celibate from choice. She snuggled closer to him. "Poor you," she said, running her hand over his chest. "I wish there was no war and I was leading you hand in hand into the woods." She opened the buttons of her shirt and edged her breasts towards him. "You're very handsome. . . . Terribly strong. . . . I bet the people you've been living with didn't find you a sweetheart."

So that was it. He shoved her with a violence that sent her sprawling across the floor. He yelled for the sentry, and when the cell door was opened he pushed her through it. "Take this slut away!" he shouted. "English pig!" she screamed back.

Slowly his rage ebbed away. In its place came a great emptiness, an emotional void.

He was given breakfast, and sat in the courtyard until mid-afternoon, when he was sent for by Fiorentini. "I have my usual question," he said. "Are you ready to tell me where you have been living? As a matter of fact it doesn't really matter whether you do or don't. We already know."

Wilde replied that in that case it was pointless to say anything—particularly since the colonel knew details of something that had never happened.

"I see," said Fiorentini. "Then please open your mouth as wide as you can." He beckoned to the guard.

Instinctively Wilde tensed himself to make a fight of it, recalling Pietro's stories of teeth being extracted without anæsthetic. He sat motionless for a moment, until, acknowledging that resistance would only increase the pain, he slowly opened his mouth. The sweat ran down his face. To his relief, the guard merely took his front upper and lower teeth one by one between his fingers and pulled firmly. "They're all his, sir," he reported. "None are false."

"So you are *not* Captain Jim. You are not the spy we are looking for; the Englishman with the dentures," Fiorentini murmured. "That means we are looking for three lots of people, not one. We want Captain Jim and the people who have been harbouring him, and the people who have been harbouring you.... And, in good time, we shall find them all."

The discovery that Wilde was not Captain Jim softened Fiorentini's attitude. "Make sure this man is given facilities to shave every day," he told the guard. "And tell the sergeant-major he is to be allowed to work in the cookhouse and have his meals there.... The same meals as the rest of you."

Late that night Wilde found his cell had been swept and provided with freshly laundered sheets. There was also a soft pillow from the cook's wife. He was able to fall asleep quickly for the first time since he surrendered, even though his last thoughts were that it could all be part of some new form of trickery, and that even if he were not the Captain Jim Fiorentini had been searching for, it in no way altered the fact that he was a prisoner and that the Bertis were still in grave danger from having hidden him.

Next morning Wilde washed his shirt under the courtyard tap, left it to dry in the sun, and went to work in the kitchen. Soon he and the cook were exchanging reminiscences of service life and were on their way to becoming firm friends. After the midday meal he joined the off-duty *fascisti* sleeping or sunbathing in the courtyard. Like the cook, they were soon asking about life in England and conditions in the Royal

Navy. It seemed the beginning of a relaxed afternoon—until the guard with whom Wilde had clashed over the cell door came through the main gate. He had been drinking and was looking for trouble.

He began by calling Wilde a string of filthy names, then started bragging about what he would do to any stupid Englishman who fell into his hands. Each sentence was punctuated with a great deal of spitting. To his disappointment, Wilde remained calm, contenting himself with occasional, and quiet, repartee. This caused the man's mood to change from one of studied insult to rage. But Wilde still smiled, and continued to reply with gentle, mocking taunts.

Suddenly the Italian lurched forward and struck Wilde on the face. This was met by the same bland smile. Then Wilde turned to the other *fascisti* and said: "He wouldn't be so fortunate if he was on his own. But if I'm fool enough to retaliate I suppose I'll be shot on the spot."

Fortunately, one of the onlookers had a sporting instinct. "Why not let them fight it out?" he asked—which was exactly what Wilde had been hoping for. The Italian dropped his uniform jacket to the ground. The man was no coward, and without further preamble the two men were at each other, no holds barred.

It was a whirlwind battle, with no pauses or interruptions, except when one man, then the other, picked himself up from the ground. At first honours were even, but soon Wilde's skill and stamina showed themselves. After a quarter of an hour's non-stop fighting, with each of them having been floored four or five times, Wilde had reached the point where he could duck or dodge nine out of ten of the Italian's swinging blows. At the same time he was able to land every blow exactly where and when he chose.

"I knew I couldn't lose," says Wilde, "but I didn't want victory to come too quickly. I hit him on the mouth, feinted for the solar plexus—but struck him again on the mouth, which was now spongy and bleeding. Then I hit him in the solar plexus in earnest, burying what seemed to be the whole of my forearm beneath the man's ribs. His head came forward, and I landed a left to the chin, hard enough to rattle his teeth, but deliberately not a knock-out punch. He straightened up and found the strength to land a left and a right to my chest. They hurt—but I knew nothing could stop me now.

"But my hatred of the man had disappeared, and I almost had to force myself to sink two lefts and a right into the Italian's cut, swollen, and messy left eye. And as I squared myself for the next attack I could feel his blood dripping from my knuckles.

"I swung a left to his temple, which made him stagger sideways and almost lose balance. Then a right to the heart—and I felt I'd never hit anyone so hard in all my life. That did it. The Italian gasped and coughed, his tongue protruded from his mouth, and his cheeks turned blue. His hands dropped to his sides, and he was virtually out on his feet.

"Drawing back, I placed the final right to his chin. It was not as hard as the previous blow, but was enough. I saw his head go back. His knees bent, and he fell forwards. The impact of his skull on the cobbles seemed to echo from the walls."

It needed many buckets of water to revive him. Wilde refreshed himself at the tap and went to bed. He ached in every joint, and had no confidence that the raw meat which the cook applied to his right eye would prevent it from becoming a monumental shiner. But it was the only mark on him. . . .

The next three days were uneventful, but boring. "My naval training stood me in good stead," Wilde recalls. "After years of keeping monotonous, seemingly interminable four-hour watches I was able to sink into a sort of trance where I was neither awake nor asleep, yet able to come alert and responsive at a second's notice. My thought processes were in a state of suspension, as it were. If it weren't for this I'd have either gone mad or done something stupid, like attempting to escape—for it was terribly frustrating to be separated by only a railing from the everyday world of the via Cavour. And I knew I could not think of escape until I was certain the Bertis were safe. For this reason I was glad my attempt to escape from the cell had come to nothing."

His next interrogator was an Italian air force officer. He began by shaking hands with Wilde, and told him he was a good soldier for escaping in order to be of further use to his country. He added that Wilde was a brave gentleman for surrendering to save other people unpleasantness. . . . As he continued he slipped an occasional question into the barrage of compliments. Wilde admired the skill with which it was done, but succeeded in answering only the harmless questions, and maintained his denial of ever having been housed by any Italian family.

The next day began ominously. He was washing at the tap when he saw a young soldier, a newcomer to the barracks, cross the courtyard towards him. Wilde felt a mounting wave of panic, for he recognized him as a visitor to neighbours of the Bertis. But there was nowhere to run to. He could only hope the soldier had a poor memory.

Half-way through the morning a guard told him the air force officer would like to interview him further. The examination began amiably enough. "Good morning, Wilde. Would you like a cigarette? How are you feeling today? Are you still getting enough to eat?" In the same casual voice he changed the subject. "Outside the door I have a soldier who knows you. He also knows the address of the family who have been hiding you."

"Although I had been expecting this," says Wilde, "I could not stop myself feeling sick and dizzy. At first I tried to ignore what had been said, but the officer just sat and waited. Finally I said, with some attempt at bravado, 'So how does that affect me?'"

The officer got up from the desk, walked to the window, and stood with his back to Wilde. "If you decide to give me the name and address of these people I shall treat them with leniency."

"I don't know what you mean," said Wilde, desperately needing time to think.

"Although I know the names and address I'd really like to

hear them from you. If you would be kind enough to give me this small satisfaction I'll merely call the people to this office, give them a severe dressing down, and leave it at that. On the other hand, if you remain silent I'm left with no choice but to do things the hard way. I'm afraid I shall have their house burned down, and they will be brought here and suffer tenfold. You must make your decision quickly.'

Says Wilde: "I was quite unable to give my thoughts any semblance of sanity or order. My brain was a confused, throbbing turmoil. Ludicrously, the only positive thing of which I was aware was the ticking of the wall clock. My body was tense and aching as I stared at the officer's back."

Minutes elapsed. Then the air force officer asked: "Well, what is your decision? I have given you a lot of time."

"It is impossible for me to say anything, because there is nothing to say."

A sigh. Then: "Don't be silly. I shall give you another five minutes. Be sensible."

Precisely five minutes later the officer repeated his question. Wilde repeated his reply. The officer walked over to the door and called out: "You did say it was Number One, didn't you?" The young soldier's voice answered, "Yes."

"Well?" asked the officer.

Wilde capitulated. His position was impossible. "Will you give me your word of honour not to ill-treat these people?"

"As one soldier to another I give you my word not to harm your friends." The officer offered Wilde his hand. Slowly, reluctantly, Wilde took it. He felt his eyes fill with tears. His voice was a sob as he gave the Bertis' name and address.

Says Wilde: "Even as I uttered the words I felt a Judas. The tears poured down my cheeks. I asked if I could see the Bertis, but was told—in that same cultured, reasoned, amiable manner—that it would not be possible. My world seemed to have come to an end. I was taken back to my cell, and cursed myself over and over for being so weak-willed. I had been tricked. Of that I was convinced. If only I'd had the sense to stick to my story. Yet there was the soldier. I didn't know what to think; but my remorse and self-recrimination were endless."

The next two days passed quietly. Either no move had been made to arrest Teresa and Giuseppe or they had been taken into custody elsewhere. The only excitement in the via Cavour was the passing of the lorries and caravans of the Ascension week fair. In the evening the clanking of the mechanical music filtered across from the fairground. To Wilde it was a dirge.

On Saturday afternoon, ten days after his arrest, an incident occurred which was to precipitate events in a most dramatic manner. Wilde was sitting in the courtyard with a group of soldiers when another soldier arrived and began talking to the tall, gaunt corporal whom Wilde had spoken to when he gave himself up. They conversed in Vogherese so that Wilde would not understand what they were discussing. (During the whole of his time at the via Cavour he had carefully avoided giving any indication that he understood a word of the dialect that was so radically different from orthodox Italian.)

As he listened he found it difficult to hide his emotions. It appeared that on the following Monday he was to be put on a prisoner-of-war train and sent to Germany. As soon as he had gone a car would be sent for the Bertis.

"The news meant only one thing," says Wilde. "I had some thirty-six hours in which to escape and warn the Bertis."

Chapter
FIVE

The Farm at Pozzol Groppo

THAT night Wilde pleaded tiredness and went early to his cell. He lay and paced in the darkness, considering idea after idea, until a plan evolved in his mind. It had many loopholes and depended far too much upon good luck, but it was the only scheme he could think of that offered any possible success.

Next morning he made a point of joking with the cook over their *caffé e latte*: it was essential for Wilde's plan that he should be in a good mood. After breakfast he offered to replenish the supply of wood stacked in a corner of the cookhouse. This meant crossing the courtyard, descending a short flight of steps, and entering a small junk-room-cum-fuel-store which was half below ground-level and half above. From a previous visit Wilde remembered seeing a chink of light at the back of the store, and it was part of his somewhat optimistic scheme that the source of light should come from outside the barracks.

He shifted the piles of cobwebbed rubbish at the back of the cellar, returning periodically to the cookhouse with a minimal load of logs. Eventually he traced the light to a small door, about two feet by three, high up the back wall. He climbed on a broken table and, singing at the top of his voice to hide the noise, managed to lever open the door a few inches, using a crowbar intended for forcing apart logs that had not been split properly. On his next journey to the cookhouse he slipped inside his shirt a large slab of butter, with which he lubricated the door's rusty hinges. Gently, apprehensively, he forced it farther and farther open. As he did so he could see his luck was holding: he glimpsed the feet of passers-by on a public highway.

It was now necessary to be permitted to stay out of his cell after dark. Apart from the dangers of escaping in daylight there was the consideration that during the afternoon and early evening on a Sunday the Bertis would probably be at Medassino. Picking his moment, he told the cook it was his birthday and that he wondered whether it would be possible to hold a small celebration that evening. The cook seemed doubtful, until Wilde told him that 250 lire, confiscated when he surrendered, had now been returned to him. He would give it all to provide a plentiful supply of *vino*.

The cook agreed. During the afternoon he went shopping on Wilde's behalf, returning with two magnums of *bianco* and one of *rosso*. The first was opened at around six o'clock, and the two men drank Wilde's health, then the cook's, then that of the cook's wife, who was away staying with friends, then the health of England, followed by Italy. They found no difficulty persuading the lone guard at the gate (the others were at the fairground) to pay frequent visits to the cookhouse for a quick glass.

At eight o'clock the guard came to take Wilde back to his cell for the night. But luck was still with him: the cook promised to lock him up later, saying he was beginning to enjoy the party and patting the Biretta revolver at his waist to indicate that he would tolerate no nonsense.

The wine disappeared rapidly, most of it down the cook's throat, the remainder behind the settee on which Wilde was sitting. Gradually the cook's speech slurred, his movements slowed, and his eyes glassed over until he was almost asleep. Cautiously Wilde eased the cook's revolver from its holster and slipped it into his own pocket: an unexpected bonus.

Now for the final stage of his plan. At washing-up time he had deliberately put to one side a large aluminium pan. Too big for the cookhouse sink, it needed to be washed in the yard. "Look, chef," said Wilde. "Fancy me leaving this dish. I'll wash it now. Then I think I'll turn in for the night."

"All right," the cook answered drowsily . . . and snored.

Making sufficient noise to attract the guard on the gate, Wilde banged the cookhouse door behind him. As the guard looked round he held up the dish and made a gesture of annoyance with a shake of his head. The guard smiled, and when Wilde turned the tap on fully, to splash as loudly as it could, he resumed his position facing the street.

Quickly Wilde bolted for the cellar, hoping the noise of the tap would hide his footsteps and that the guard would take a long time to realize that the dish needed an unconscionable amount of cleaning.

It was only seconds later that Wilde squeezed through the doorway of the store and was standing on a corner of the piazza del Castello.

Now to get to the via Sant' Ambrogio. He hurried past the fairground which adjoined the *piazza* and turned down a side-street he knew, almost knocking over a courting couple huddled in the shadows. He was just approaching the piazzetta Plana when a black car raced past.

"To my horror," says Wilde, "I saw it pull up in the shadows on the far side of the via Sant' Ambrogio. Five men jumped out and hid themselves in doorways and in the entrance of a near-by alley. The car parked round a corner out of sight. There was no mistaking the men or their purpose: they wanted to catch me on the Bertis' doorstep. Somewhere along the line my plan, which had seemed so successful, had misfired."

(In fact, Wilde had been betrayed by a freakishness of fate. The dish he had left under the tap had slipped in such a way as to block the drain completely. With the tap on full, it did not take long for the water to cascade across the courtyard past the sentry and so announce that something was amiss.)

Wilde was still debating whether to wait in the hope that the men would go away, when, after ten minutes, their patience came to an end. He saw them go to the Bertis' front door and ring the bell. As Giuseppe appeared in the lighted opening they pushed him inside and slammed the door behind them. There was nothing he could do. There was no point staying watching, but he was hypnotzied by the situation. After another twenty minutes a man left the flat and returned with the car. Teresa and Giuseppe were hustled into it and driven off with two escorts, leaving three men to wait for Wilde. He stayed where he was for a further two or three minutes, dismissing thoughts of a pointless second surrender.

He decided to tell Serafina of what had happened to the Bertis. The door of her house was locked, and for a while his knocking brought no response. Eventually Serafina's mother peered round the door, recognized him, and, despite her undisguised fear, beckoned him in. Serafina, who had been at the fair, arrived soon afterwards. She expressed little surprise at seeing him. The news of his escape was all over the town. All roads were blocked, and the authorities were making it impossible for anyone to leave.

Wilde's only concern was for Teresa and Giuseppe. For himself the issue was simple: he would succeed in escaping or would be recaptured. For the moment it did not worry him which. Although he was glad to have Serafina's assurance that he had done all anyone could, he still felt the burden of guilty responsibility.

He was about to leave, when Serafina stopped him. Where was he going? What would he do? Wilde did not know the answers; he was aware merely of the need to get away without implicating anyone else in his predicament. Serafina explained that, with the roads impassable, his only hope was the railway. For that he needed to accept her help whether he liked it or not. And if he stayed in Voghera and was recaptured, who was to tell whether it would not weigh more heavily against the Bertis? Wilde allowed himself to be persuaded.

At five in the morning Serafina went to the station, which was only a few hundred yards from the house, and came back with a return ticket for herself and a single for Wilde. The first train left at 5.45, so there was no time to spare.

They walked to the station separately, Serafina in the lead.

A uniformed member of the Brigata Nera was standing by the ticket window, but the gate to the platform was manned only by the ticket-collector. Aboard the train they managed to find an empty compartment.

The little two-coach train was bound for Varzi, a small town some twenty-five miles south-east of Voghera, along the valley of the river Staffora. Half-way between the two, where the hills began to close in tightly on the triple ribbon of road, river, and rail, lay the tiny village of Godiasco. It was the train's first stop and their own destination. Relatives of Serafina lived near Godiasco, and she was certain they would either hide Wilde or pass him to a place of greater safety.

They were visited by a ticket-inspector, who bade them a very good morning, but showed no special interest in either them or their tickets. Wilde could not prevent himself expecting trouble at every turn and whenever anyone moved along the corridor he pressed his elbow against his revolver to give himself some measure of reassurance.

But they arrived at Godiasco without incident, and alighted from the train to the welcome of a heavy thunderstorm. They crossed the river at the village bridge, and began to walk along the winding, narrow road that traversed the hilly farmland before zigzagging up the mountain-side. The rain came down in a savage, unbroken sheet. Serafina was protected to some extent by her trench coat, but Wilde, wearing only the shirt, jacket, and trousers in which he had surrendered, was drenched.

They had about nine miles of rugged mountain road to cover, so did not have time to shelter until the rain had stopped. But Wilde would like it when he got there, Serafina assured him. Yes, he was bound to like Pozzol Groppo.

In Voghera the Bertis were now in the Castello. They were locked in separate underground cells, their only source of light and air the heavily grilled V-shaped slits that opened on to the *piazza* above. They were not so see each other for the entire period of their imprisonment.

The separation apart, Teresa was well treated. Giuseppe,

on the other hand, had to endure frequent and savage beatings during the first fortnight after his capture. The stated purpose of the beatings was to persuade him to reveal where Wilde was now hiding—but it soon became clear that he was being whipped across the back and struck across the face for the sheer pleasure it gave his guards. There was also an element of released frustration: the Fascist authorities felt that Wilde's long sojourn in the town had made them the laughing-stock not only of the townspeople, but also of their colleagues the Germans.

After the first fortnight Teresa and Giuseppe were treated far better than the deliberately circulated rumours would have had the people of Voghera believe. To keep anti-Fascist and anti-German activities in check Pastorelli's staff spread stories of atrocious punishments being meted out to "the traitors of the via Sant' Ambrogio." It was sound psychological warfare, and to a great extent it worked.

The Bertis' imprisonment in the Castello continued from June until almost the end of the year, when they were moved to Milan. There they remained until the end of hostilities in May 1945.

The one remarkable feature of their imprisonment was that no effort was made to discover from them the names of other people who had helped Wilde. Serafina and her mother were never approached; and, although Medassino was subjected to close scrutiny, the Morinis—despite their being related to the Bertis—were asked no more than a few simple questions. Their denial of any knowledge of Wilde was immediately accepted. It seemed, too, that the Brigata Nera were still satisfied of Pietro's innocence, for no further attempts were made to question him.

The Rovatis were less fortunate. A few days after Wilde's escape notices were posted offering a reward for information about the *scappato Inglese*.

Someone talked—reported that the Englishman had been seen with the Rovatis. A detachment of twelve Blackshirts, led by a captain, came to the little farm and questioned Frederico. They said they were satisfied that he had no knowledge of the Englishman's present whereabouts, and for this reason would not take him off to prison. They would treat him with extreme leniency. This involved taking him round to the back of the farmhouse and beating him unconscious with the butts of their rifles.

Some of the house-to-house questioning in Medassino was led by Fiorentini. One man he was anxious to talk to was Egidio Ferretti. When he learned they were after him Ferretti decided to take a trip. By bicycle he first went to Alessandria . . . then to Acqui Terme . . . on to Bistagno, a little town west of Turin and some sixty miles from Medassino. He was away for about five weeks before returning—secretly—to see whether he was still being searched for. As ill-fortune had it, he was recognized by a soldier as he approached the outskirts of Medassino. The guard was also on a bicycle, and there was a furious chase down the country lanes, with Ferretti's greater fitness (or more modern machine) winning the day. He returned to Bistagno.

He managed to let his family know his address, and learned that Fiorentini had arrested his sixty-year-old father in his place. Ferretti could not abandon his father. He rode to Voghera and surrendered at the via Cavour.

His interrogation was prolonged, but not particularly unpleasant. It took him some considerable time to convince Fiorentini that his absence from Medassino was not connected with Wilde's disappearance, particularly since it seemed to be known that Ferretti had been responsible for taking Wilde up into the hills the previous autumn. His father was released, and Ferretti was freed a week later. Fiorentini had learned nothing, and Ferretti had gained an heroic reputation.

After almost three hours' climbing Serafina and Wilde arrived at the cluster of half a dozen houses that was Pozzol Groppo. The name of the hamlet was also that of the surrounding mountains, and in this latter capacity was of some importance to the geography of the Voghera–Varzi area.

While Serafina went to talk to her cousin Wilde stood for

about five minutes unable to control the shivering of his body or the chattering of his teeth: his body cooled rapidly when he stopped walking, and the wetness of his clothes made him feel as though he had just stepped from an ice-cold bath.

It did not take Wilde long to recognize the hostility in the faces of Serafina's cousin and her husband. With hardly enough time to thank Serafina and say goodbye to her he was hurried upstairs to a tiny attic. He looked longingly at the roaring log fire in the living-room, but they urged him along, determined to get him hidden away as soon as possible.

Before leaving him they issued instructions: he was to keep completely out of sight . . . he was never to leave the room . . . he was not to smoke . . . and there were several other do's and don't's. "I was on the edge of losing my temper," says Wilde, "but as soon as I stripped off my clothes and settled in bed I was able to remind myself that these people had absolutely no reason in the world to undergo even the slightest risk on my behalf. I meant nothing to them. It was extremely kind of them to be doing what they were doing. And I could think of many families I knew in England who would not do this much in similar circumstances. And what right had I to expect help?"

Wilde slept. It was dark when he awoke, to hear the sound of footsteps on the stairs. A man's voice told him to dress and come down as quickly as he could. It was a stranger's voice —but when he went down to the living-room Wilde saw only his hosts. Although it was the middle of the night they had bread and soup for him, and refused to answer questions about the stranger until he had eaten. Then they told him a man was waiting out in the barn.

At the door of the barn Wilde was greeted with a highly accented English: "I am a friend." Wilde answered in his fluent Italian, and the stranger laughed. "If I'd known I wouldn't have spent an hour perfecting my English phrases."

Inside the barn was a small hurricane lamp, and by it Wilde could see that his companion was in his early twenties, immaculately—almost foppishly—dressed. He introduced himself as Domenico.

He was another of Serafina's cousins, and had been working in a bank at Milan until being dismissed for his pro-British sympathies. He lived with his parents in a house about half a mile away from the hamlet proper. He said that what he had to offer was not as comfortable as the house Wilde had just left—but he was a willing host. He suggested that Wilde should hide by day in a local wood and have his meals brought to him there by Domenico. At night he would sleep among the bundles of hay in the barn of Domenico's father. To Wilde it was reminiscent of the previous September when he had been housed in Pietro's nephew's barn. "As I walked along with Domenico," says Wilde, "I felt that I was on the brink of something positive at last. That I was on the verge of finally justifying myself."

His first meal in the woods was attended by no less than five people. Domenico introduced the four newcomers, solemnly adding their ages to their names: his sister Ernestina (forty-six), his sister Rosetta (twenty-eight), his brothers Agostino (thirty-five) and Luigi (nineteen). It was quite clear that Agostino resented Wilde's presence, but it was equally clear that Domenico was considered the genius of the family—after all, hadn't he worked in a bank in the big city?—and that he was allowed to have his way in most family decisions.

After a week Wilde was invited to eat in the house of Domenico's uncle, who owned the largest farm in the district and was the acknowledged head of the clan. The invitation followed a visit Domenico had made to Voghera, where he learned that a large reward was being offered for information leading to Wilde's recapture. This, according to Domenico's uncle, was fame of a high order, and meant that the Englishman was worthy of recognition.

The days passed slowly. Some days Wilde would lie in the woods, dozing the hours away. On others he would work on Domenico's uncle's or father's farm, spraying vines with a foul-smelling insecticide from a canister strapped to his back.

This apparatus was virtually the only element of mechanization on the farms. There was no agricultural land of quality, and even marginal land was scarce. But for centuries the farmers of Pozzol Groppo had clung to their almost barren hillsides, stubbornly retaining the customs and habits of earlier generations. The people were industrious—had to be in order to scrape some sort of livelihood from the soil—and formed a community in which the spade, hoe, and axe were the only agricultural implements; where crops were left, fatalistically, to the whims of the elements; where the *padrone*'s pair of oxen was hired for ploughing and harvesting; and where exchange in kind almost obviated the need for money. But they were content in that they were independent: no matter how meagre their crops and how primitive their standard of living, they were their own masters. Olives, grapes, potatoes, and irregular crops of maize were the products of the area, although a little grass was cultivated for the few milk cattle. And at least there was plenty of local timber for housing needs.

Although Wilde would have given a great deal for news of his family and fiancée, Doreen, he was able to catch up with news of the Allied progress northward in Italy. By now Monte Cassino and the monastery had been captured, the armies had broken out from Anzio, and the Fifth Army had entered Rome. This latter victory excited Domenico and his family enormously—but Wilde did not share their enthusiasm: it was now obvious that the Germans were contesting bitterly every inch of Italian soil. By this token, even the news of the D-day landings could not be interpreted as meaning that the War was as good as over.

One evening in July, some three weeks after Wilde's arrival, the men were drinking wine at the farmhouse when they saw smoke and flames coming from the village of San Sebastiano to the south. Next morning they heard sporadic rifle and machine-gun fire from the same direction. The farmer and his family knew what had happened; in San Sebastiano, they told Wilde, some of the villagers' sons would have refused to enrol to help fight the partisans, and the

Fascist recruiting party would be burning their farms and shooting the cattle. It was a regular occurrence.

During the afternoon of the following day two men passed close to Wilde's hideout in the woods. He followed them at a distance as they made their way to the farm of Domenico's father. They were curiously dressed. One wore a German drill cap, a short black reefer jacket, a red scarf round his waist, and what appeared to be German jackboots. The other wore parachutist-style camouflage jacket and trousers and had a large stetson on his head. Both carried revolvers.

When they spoke to Domenico he approached as near as he dared, and managed to catch the word *partigiani*. So here, at last, were his first partisans. He thought of rushing out and introducing himself—then decided it would be better to wait and see if Domenico summoned him. The two men stayed for about an hour, talking with Domenico and drinking his wine.

As soon as they had gone Domenico ran to the woods to tell Wilde that they, like the *fascisti*, were recruiting for volunteers. The difference was that they wanted genuine volunteers: the life would be dangerous and rough. They had occupied San Sebastiano within an hour of the Blackshirts' departure, and it was there that volunteers should report within the next four days.

So it had happened at last. "There was no need for consideration or debate," Wilde recalls. "This was it. It had taken a long time coming, but at last I was going to play some active part in the War again. At last I was going to justify my months on the run. Once again life held some positive purpose. I felt terribly excited and impatient."

Domenico told Wilde he would come with him—although he was worried. Not about the danger, but the hardiness of the partisans' life. He had never been strong—he did not pass his medical for military service—and doubted whether he'd be able to keep up with his comrades. But he'd try. Neither Agostino nor Luigi was prepared to leave Pozzol Groppo, first arguing the need to stay and look after the farm, then admitting that they thought partisan life too stupid and suicidal to warrant serious consideration. They begged Domenico to remain, and swore at Wilde for setting such a criminally dangerous example. But their brother was adamant.

Next day they left for San Sebastiano. They had to cover nine miles across country, negotiating narrow mountain goat-tracks before descending to the valley of the river Curone. They had not left Pozzol Groppo as early as they had planned: family farewells, Italian style, were always prolonged. So they had to hurry along in the overpowering heat of the afternoon. It took five hours to reach the outskirts of the village, and Wilde realized that he was badly out of condition. Domenico, however, was suffering far more severely, and Wilde doubted whether his companion would ever be tough enough for the life ahead. For himself, he knew it would not be long before he returned to maximum fitness.

As they entered the village he found himself wondering just how successfully he would adapt himself to the partisan way of life. If he had known the answer he would have been amazed.

Chapter
SIX

The Camp above Dernice

DURING his stay at Pozzol Groppo, more to pass the time than anything else, Wilde had studied and memorized a map of the area. The main trunk road south from Milan to Genoa passed through Voghera. From Genoa the road ran south-east along the coast through the small resorts of Rapallo and Chiavari to the naval base at La Spezia, then on to Pisa, Florence, and Rome. But there was an alternative route. It turned off from the trunk road at Voghera, ran along the valley of the Staffora as far as Varzi, then climbed the twisting Penice Pass through a shoulder of the Apennines, before bending south towards the coast some forty miles away. This second road was much used by German military traffic, and its vantage-points were heavily defended.

Parallel to the valley of the Staffora ran the valley of the Curone. But the road that followed this valley led nowhere. It wandered about fifteen miles south-east of San Sebastiano, serving small hamlets and lonely farms scattered with increasing infrequency as the road twisted deeper into the mountains. From it an occasional minor road branched northward and eastward to the Varzi road, or southward and westward to the richer and more populous province of Alessandria.

That part of the Emilian Apennines in which lie Varzi and San Sebastiano is known for its rough, rugged, and desolate landscape. It is mountain country, with peaks rising to above four thousand feet and many roads climbing to more than three thousand. High up it is a scene of rocky outcrops jostling crowded pine forests. On the protected and south-facing upper slopes the surface is broken with patches of farmland, the edges of the fields planted with conifers to serve as windbreaks.

Lower down the slopes the dominant feature is the land's dryness. Great areas of bare, dusty brown occasionally give way to thin, yellow grass and stunted shrubs. The only fertile parts are the narrow river valleys and the few wet upper slopes, where are to be found the orchards, the vineyards, and the pasture. There are rare patches where maize can be grown, but grass for wintering the draught oxen is a more common sight than corn. But farmland of any type is sparse and poor. Even the lower reaches of the Staffora and Curone valleys suffer badly in the summer: the two rivers dwindle into sluggish and narrow ribbons of shallow water trickling between carpets of smooth grey stones that stretch heartbreakingly across the broad winter beds.

It is a forbidding yet imposing landscape, and an apparent irony that so desolate an area can exist within fifty miles of Milan and forty of Genoa. But its natural characteristics make it immune from development or progress. Today, as in the War years, it is little penetrated by tourists, or even by Italians of its own province.

This, then, was the countryside through which Wilde and Domenico travelled. At San Sebastiano they were stopped at two road blocks before they reached the village square. Each block was manned by half a dozen partisans, wearing a variegated rag-bag of costume and leaning lazily on rifles or gesturing grandiloquently with *mitra* sub-machine guns. At each block the news that Wilde was English produced a dramatic and unusually polite response—swagger and coarseness of tongue were a hallmark of the *partigiani*. Wilde was addressed as *signore*—a rare mark of respect.

In the village square Wilde asked where he could find the partisans' leader. He was told he was known as Chiri-ci-chi, but was away fighting in another part of the mountains. In any case, he and Domenico were to be sent to a training camp in the hills. They were told to get a meal at a near-by *albergo*. Then a guide would take the day's volunteers to the camp.

As they sat eating on the terrace of the inn they watched a scene of increasing—and often apparently purposeless—activity. Groups of partisans came and went between the road blocks and observation points in the hills. A patrol of about twenty men lined up with no pretence at military precision and set off eastward along the valley. Two ox-carts were loaded with bread and vegetables. The sides of the square were lined with villagers watching the activity, and bidding noisy farewells to the group of young volunteers who were to be Wilde's companions. Some, he saw, were full of noise and bravado; others were apprehensive, licking their lips as though wondering what they had let themselves in for; a few stood silent and impassive.

"For my part," says Wilde, "excitement and impatience still dominated my emotions. I wanted to march off there and then—although I'd no idea where to—and kill Germans. I felt supremely confident and powerful. Thinking back, I don't believe these emotions were inspired by bloodthirstiness on my part. Rather it was the release of an enormous amount of bottled-up emotion: a chance to play—to some extent—the rôle of the hunter instead of the hunted."

They left the village at about five-thirty that evening, and followed a winding side-road to a hamlet called Dernice, before turning off across country. It was a complicated route, and Wilde soon abandoned any attempt to memorize it. They were climbing steadily, and it took two and a half hours from San Sebastiano to reach the camp.

It was a compact, grassy clearing, framed with pine-trees and set in the curve of a rock wall. Four small tents had been erected, and another four were on the ground waiting to be assembled. It was clear, however, that most people would have to sleep in the open; the group squatting around the blazing fire for their evening meal numbered about forty, while the day's recruits added a further ten.

In the manner of recruits the world over, the newcomers

kept in the background, Wilde and Domenico sprawled on the grass. The sailor was accustomed to rough living, but he felt that the former bank clerk was quite disgusted by the overall crudeness of the men round the fire. When the old hands had finished eating, the new recruits were summoned to collect their plates of meat stew. Each was given a dirty dish and spoon, and Wilde and Domenico were the only ones to go in search of a bucket of water in which to wash them. As they did so a tall, bearded partisan came over.

"Why are you washing the plates?" he asked aggressively.

"I never ate from anyone else's plate in prison camp," said Wilde, "and I'm certainly not going to start now."

The man sneered. "You are a stupid English bastard," he said, then spat at Wilde's feet before turning, grinning, towards his friends.

This was clearly intended as a challenge. Within seconds most of the men had gathered to see what would happen. Wilde took his time and waited theatrically for his audience to be settled. Then he walked straight up to the man and without a word smashed his hand so hard in his mouth that he was knocked completely off his feet. He pulled himself up slowly into a sitting position, shook his head, and spat blood. But it was all over; it was plain that he did not intend making a fight of it. Wilde looked down at him and, speaking calmly —but loud enough for everyone to hear—told his adversary to *sta in gamba* (watch out for himself). Then he picked up his spoon and plate, put his arm round Domenico's shoulder, and walked across to collect his supper.

Says Wilde: "I spent the night under the stars, with my coat as a pillow. All manner of thoughts jostled one another in my mind, but here again my years in the Navy came to my aid. I was able to shut my mind to them and go to sleep."

He was awakened in the early hours of the morning by the sound of artillery fire. As he lay in his hollowed-out bed of grass beneath a pine-tree he could place the direction, but assumed from the absence of gun-flash that the engagement was some distance away. Only one person other than himself seemed to be on his feet and interested in the gunfire, and Wilde went over to him. It was the guide who had brought them from San Sebastiano. He told Wilde that there was fighting in the mountains near Serravalle, a pass through which ran the main Milan–Genoa trunk road and which commanded the vital road and rail junction of Novi Ligure. A partisan group had been occupying this hazardous and ambitious position for some days, and action with the Germans in the area flared up about once a day. The pass was about ten miles away on the map, but two ranges of mountains lay between, and there was no road. This was all he knew—and apparently all he cared.

"I felt furious at this apathy," says Wilde. "By now dawn was breaking, and I thought it was about time I not only met the camp commander but asked him what he was going to do to help his comrades."

Wilde pushed open the flap of his tent and found himself watching a man and woman making love under a torn blanket. He muttered an apology and started to leave, but the man roared at him to come back.

"Stay. Speak up. What is it? What do you want? What's the matter?" He sat upright, leaving the woman to pull the blanket hastily over herself.

He was a short, broad figure of a man aged about thirty, his head, chest, arms, and stomach thickly covered with black hair. The woman was about ten years younger. She seemed the taller of the two—as far as Wilde could judge—and with her pale face, aquiline nose, and long hair gave the appearance of a traditional northern Italian beauty. She also appeared to have an excellent figure.

In his embarrassment Wilde blurted out, "I am an Englishman, and would appreciate some sort of attention." As he uttered the words he realized how pompous he must have sounded—and that he had no idea of the attention he wanted.

The little man jumped from the bed and shouted, "An Englishman! Bravo! Bravo!" He shook Wilde warmly by the hand, and bounced around the tent, dragging Wilde with him as he continued to pump his arm up and down. Finally he released his grip and, to the accompaniment of further bravos, pulled on a pair of trousers.

He asked for Wilde's history. The Englishman gave it to him—albeit with some difficulty, since the partisan continually interrupted with a barrage of questions, congratulations, and enthusiastic bravos. As soon as Wilde had finished he started to tell him of the success of the recruiting drive for which he was responsible. Of the fifty men in the camp twenty were experienced partisans; the rest had arrived via San Sebastiano during the past week. Wilde also gathered that the man's name was Cesare, his companion's Maria. These appeared to be real names, not the *noms de guerre* adopted by most partisans and designed to make it impossible for their comrades to reveal their true identities in the event of being captured and tortured.

At first Maria succeeded in keeping the blanket to neck-level. Then, as Cesare turned from the subject of recruiting to an account of actions in which he had taken part during recent months, her arms became tired—or she felt there was no need for false modesty in front of Wilde. The covering slipped lower and lower, until it served absolutely no purpose at all—and Wilde found it increasingly difficult to concentrate on Cesare's recitation of achievements.

Finally Wilde felt he had heard enough of the past and wanted to know something of the present and future. He asked about the battle waging at Serravalle. Cesare told him that Chiri-ci-chi was leading a force of about two hundred and fifty partisans there, and was engaged by five or six hundred Germans, supported by a further hundred *fascisti*. Before this action partisan activity in the hills had been confined to the remoter Apennines: the current expedition against the main trunk road was by far the most ambitious venture they had attempted.

On the first night of the battle Chiri-ci-chi's force had made a number of successful surprise attacks, and had accounted for about thirty enemy vehicles and twice as many men. The counter-attack this provoked had proved to be much larger than the partisans had anticipated, or previously experienced. Now they were retreating deeper into the mountains—the advantage theirs. For they knew the subtleties and secrets of the terrain, and when their better equipped and more heavily armed opponents were poised to finish them off the partisans could melt away and disappear into the mountains. In the meantime, because of the nature of the fighting, they were able to inflict heavy casualties on the enemy as they retreated.

Cesare returned to the subject of recruitment. His task, he explained, was to gather volunteers, give them the barest amount of training, then send them to fill the gaps the present battle would make in the forces of Chiri-ci-chi. Then, in mid-sentence, he broke off . . . stared hard at Wilde . . . gave a mighty bellow . . . and dropped his bombshell.

"You are an Englishman. You must know all about fighting. I stand down. You are now in complete charge. Bravo!"

"I was so astonished," says Wilde, "that I couldn't think of anything to say. I started to mutter something, but Cesare shouted me down with, 'You will have this tent. It is the commandant's tent. I will throw that pig of a Venetian out of the tent next door. He should never have had one to himself, anyway.'

"I tried to explain that I was an ordinary sailor, not even an officer, who knew something about the inside of a submarine, but nothing about guerrilla warfare—Cesare just shouted me down. There was no arguing with him . . . and suddenly there seemed to be a curious inevitability about it all. Call it fate, or whatever you like, but I was convinced that I *should* take over. It now appeared to be the most natural thing in the world.

"But *how* would I take over? The answer to that was another question: in the same circumstances what would John Bromage, the skipper of *Sahib*, have done?"

Wilde thought for a while before telling Cesare: "Summon the men. Tell them I am in command, and then I will talk to them."

Fortunately, Cesare's announcement was greeted with

enthusiasm. "That was the strangest thing of all," Wilde recalls. "Nobody seemed in the least surprised—even the man I'd hit the previous evening joined in the cheering. It had the surrealist quality of a mad dream."

Wilde issued his orders. They would strike camp at midnight. Tents and unnecessary equipment, such as cooking utensils, would be left behind, well hidden. They would plan to reach Chiri-ci-chi's force as early as possible next day. As far as today was concerned, it would be spent giving the newcomers weapon-training. (Most, anyway, were experienced huntsmen who knew how to aim and fire a gun.) The others would spend the morning checking arms and ammunition. Everyone should try to get some sleep during the afternoon and early evening. Finally, any man who'd had second thoughts about joining the partisans would be allowed to return home without any reflection on his character. There was only one question from the men: could they have more details of the night's operation? Wilde said he would brief them more fully later in the day.

"As the morning wore on," says Wilde, "the most extraordinary thing was that I really did feel like a commanding officer—not a helpless Able Seaman stuck in the middle of the Italian mountains grappling with something I couldn't pretend to understand. It was extraordinary—but immensely satisfying."

At about noon Domenico came up to him. Embarrassed, his head on his chest, he said that he would prefer not to accompany the partisans that night. He felt it would be better if he went home and tried to serve in some capacity in which physical strength was not a necessary ingredient. Wilde assured him that he understood. He watched him negotiate the footpath from the camp, hoping he would not lose his way—he was the only volunteer to be returning—and felt very alone and sad.

Later the youngest in the group who had come from San Sebastiano approached Wilde. He looked almost as embarrassed as Domenico. "Please . . . please may I stay with you all the time during the battle tomorrow?" he asked.

"Of course," Wilde replied. "But why?"

"Because I'm afraid. I'm terribly scared. But . . . but please don't tell the others. They'd laugh at me."

"I promise. But why don't you go home?"

"I'm an orphan. I've no real home to go to."

The boy's name was Eugenio, and he was fifteen years old. Wilde appointed him his personal messenger.

As he walked round the camp Wilde looked carefully for any sign of anxiety or discontent about the night's march to Chiri-ci-chi. To any man who seemed to hold any doubts he explained that this, after all, was what they had joined the partisans to do, and that any man who wished to leave could still do so. Finally, after a period of instruction on the *mitra*, eight men decided they would like to go back to their farms. Without exception they looked shamefaced as they walked from the camp, and Wilde, who was able to understand their change of heart, spoke sharply to one of the veterans who spat at them as they went past.

He inspected the camp's stock of arms and ammunition. There was an assortment of rifles of a variety of different makes, eight *mitras*, a dozen revolvers, and fifty German stick-grenades. Wilde already had the revolver he had taken from the via Cavour, but Cesare also insisted on him accepting one of his personal revolvers: a German officer's P 38, with two clips and fifty rounds of ammunition. It fired the same type of bullet as the *mitra*, which was of practical value. There was no holster for it, so he squatted on the grass and spliced a seaman's long lanyard to the butt, passing the loop round his neck and tucking the gun into the top of his trousers. His dexterity with the intricacies of the splice brought widespread congratulations, and he had to promise to make lanyards for the rest of the men as soon as he had time.

Before the partisans settled down for a few hours' rest Wilde gave them details of the plan he had worked out during the day. First he wanted volunteers for an advance party. Seven men stepped forward, and he selected five of them. They would leave an hour earlier, at eleven o'clock, to scout for enemy patrols along the proposed line of advance. If a patrol was spotted one of the five would hasten back to the main body of the partisans, while the other four would keep the Germans under observation. In no circumstances, however, would the patrol advance farther than the main road that ran parallel to the San Sebastiano road. Once they reached this road they would take cover and keep their eyes open for enemy movements along it.

Everything seemed organized, Wilde told himself. It was now seven o'clock. At ten the partisans would have a late supper of wine, cold meat, and cheese; in the meantime he would sleep. But as he was about to settle down in his tent a thought struck him. What was to happen to Maria? He should have sent her to San Sebastiano with the eight men who returned home. But what if she didn't come from San Sebastiano? . . . A forced march with a battle at the end of it was no situation for a woman. He sent for Cesare.

The partisan expressed astonishment. "Maria is mine," he said. "Sometimes she may look like this" (his hands described an improbably huge bosom), "but she is mine, and everywhere I go she goes. Anyway, she is better in the mountains than most of the men. She is good with a gun." He leaned forward confidentially. "Most of the killings I told you about this morning were hers, not mine. She lets me pretend about them because she knows I like to play the hero." Wilde thought he could see Cesare grin in the darkness of the tent before raising the flap and scuttling out.

He returned some minutes later with Maria. She was dressed in khaki shirt and trousers, with a long scarf round her hair. She wore heavy climbing boots. Across her shoulders was slung a *mitra*, and a long hunting-knife was sheathed at her waist. The one incongruous touch, Wilde thought, was the rosary at her neck. He agreed with Cesare that Maria looked every inch a soldier. Smiling happily, the couple walked off hand in hand into the gathering dusk.

Says Wilde: "I thought to myself, 'I hope she doesn't get killed'—and that was really the first realization that this wasn't just a game. People were not only going to shoot guns, but get shot at as well. And some were going to get hit. I didn't rest quite so well after that."

The men ate; the advance party disappeared into the night. "I was relieved when midnight came," says Wilde. "It is always better when thoughts and doubts and fears are replaced by action." The party numbered thirty-six, including Wilde. The Englishman led, accompanied by a man who came from Serravalle and who knew every inch of the territory. Eugenio kept as close to Wilde as he could, while Cesare and Maria were about half-way along the strung-out line of march.

The sky was black save for a sprinkling of stars that seemed unreally brilliant against the solid darkness. Occasionally they heard firing as they advanced, and sometimes caught sight of the flashes in the distance. The fighting was plainly closer now than it had been the previous night. The night was warm, and there was practically no breeze. They stumbled along winding goat-tracks and slid down the sides of small gullies. But for the first hour they were mostly climbing, until they slipped through a narrow gap between two towering pillars of rock and found themselves on the far side of the first ridge of peaks. They began descending towards the road thirteen hundred feet below.

By two-thirty they were more than half-way down, and rested for a few minutes beside the ruined walls of a medieval guard-tower, its original function to guard the road they were now approaching. As they sat they became aware of a noise and a tiny glow of light: a man smoking a cigarette approached. They froze into silence until he drew level. Revolver raised, Wilde stepped forward and ordered, "Stay where you are." Before the man could speak there were cries of recognition from the men in Wilde's party—he was from Chiri-ci-chi's force.

Wilde explained briefly that he had been elected Captain (the title the partisans insisted on calling him by). The newcomer said he had become separated from his patrol during a clash with a large body of Germans. Thinking it would be too difficult for one man to rejoin the main partisan force on his own, he was heading for the camp to warn them of what was happening. It amounted to this: the partisans had continued to get the worst of the battle and the Germans were still pouring in reinforcements. Soon they would have a four-to-one superiority. He was positive that Chiri-ci-chi's force would be wiped out if they fought on, and that the Germans, knowing the partisans had come from the San Sebastiano area, would sweep eastward.

"All the more reason for us to go to Chiri-ci-chi's aid," said Wilde—and the party marched onward towards Serravalle. An hour later they had reached the road and located their advance-guard. At this very moment they saw a line of headlights coming along the road towards them, and a convoy of ten lorries loaded with troops raced past. Wilde swore: had they arrived just a few minutes earlier they would have been able to open fire. As it was, they could only crouch in the shadows and watch the enemy speed by.

No sooner were the lorries out of sight than another returning partisan came out of the darkness. He was known as *Tenente* ("Lieutenant"), and was in possession of more facts than the first man had been. His news was mixed. It was good in that the casualties among the partisans were less than had been feared: a dozen killed and between thirty and forty wounded. It was bad in that there was no purpose in advancing farther: Chiri-ci-chi had decided that the counter-attack was now so large that the time had come to disappear into the mountains. He was going to move his men due south and then return via a point well below the enemy forces.

Wilde agreed reluctantly that the only thing to do was to return to camp and wait.

They arrived back at ten o'clock that morning. Wilde was so weary he could have thrown himself down there and then and slept. His exhaustion, he knew, stemmed as much from a sense of anticlimax as from physical effort. He remembered his responsibilities, and saw that breakfast was prepared and sentries posted on an hourly rota before curling under a tree and falling asleep.

Chapter
SEVEN

Journey to Castagnola

AT noon Wilde was awakened by the sound of a single rifle-shot, the agreed signal from the more distant sentries. He hurried to a vantage-point, and could see, climbing the rockface towards them, half a dozen men. One of his group produced a small pair of prismatic binoculars which he thrust into Wilde's hands, saying the *Capitano* should keep them. Wilde thanked him and focused the glasses. The men were returning partisans, so weary they could hardly drag one leg after the other. Calling those around him to follow, Wilde scrambled down the slope to meet the partisans and help them home.

Some of his men were quicker than Wilde, and must have briefly explained his position, for he was greeted with hoarse cries of *Capitano* and *Signore* and was accorded something in the nature of a salute.

One of the returning partisans had a bullet wound high on the inside of his thigh, wrapped in a dirty piece of cloth. His comrades carried him to the clearing and laid him on the grass. Wilde felt it was his duty to tend the wound, although he knew nothing of first-aid, and certainly had no idea of how to treat a bullet wound.

He made the man comfortable on folded coats and blankets and cut away his blood-soaked trousers. Fighting down his nausea, he removed the bandage as gently as he could, although he had to tug hard at those parts of it that were stuck to the flesh. The inside layers of bandage were now no more than a mass of clotting blood and sodden material. The smell was foul.

Wilde's final tug at the last of the bandaging caused the partisan to faint. He remained unconscious, and Wilde was able to clean up the wound without worrying that he might be causing pain. He remembered a childhood maxim that it was wrong to put a cut finger under a cold tap and ordered water to be boiled at the camp fire. As he bathed the wound and washed away the blood Wilde saw that it was less severe than he had supposed and that the smell was due to lack of cleanliness, not gangrene. He could see that the blood was still flowing gently from two holes—one at the front of the thigh, one at the back—and assumed the bullet had gone clean through.

Sacrificing his own clean underwear and commandeering a few handkerchieves, he made pads to put over the wound and bandages to wrap round it. He washed the rest of the man's body, and it was while he was doing this that the man regained consciousness. "Thank you," he said. "I am very grateful. I feel fine."

Says Wilde, "I still felt sick in the stomach, but my confidence had received a useful boost. The partisans seemed to see in my doctoring further evidence of my fitness to lead them, and as I walked round the camp greeting sentries and organizing meals I was met with expressions of respect and goodwill. I managed to snatch some more sleep during the afternoon, and woke to find that Eugenio had kept back for me a ration of boiled meat, potatoes, and peas from the evening meal."

Next morning Wilde conferred with the *Tenente*, who was leaving to deliver messages from Chiri-ci-chi to other partisan groups in the area. He had to liaise with the leaders at San Sebastiano before crossing to the far side of the Staffora and contacting the large brigade that operated north of Varzi in the mountains round Val di Nizza and Zavattarello Valverde. The *Tenente*'s advice was that Wilde should not take his detachment back to San Sebastiano, which he thought was now overdue for an attack from enemy troops based at

Voghera. The village, he said, had a long record of changing hands, as it seemed to represent the practical limit to which the authorities could push their area of control.

Instead he recommended that Wilde should lead his men to a place deeper into the mountains called Capannette di Pej. This was an agreed regroupment area to which isolated parties of partisans knew they could retire in the face of extreme enemy pressure, in the expectation of finding other partisans there. Because it threatened no part of the enemy communications system in the area, and because it was so far off the beaten track, it was considered immune from attack —or had been until then.

Cesare confirmed the wisdom of the advice, and Wilde called a meeting of the detachment to announce that they would leave at midnight. He spent the rest of the day getting to know better the men he was commanding. He was particularly intrigued by their *noms de guerre*, including Fuoco ("Fire"), Fulmine ("Lightning"), Terribile ("Terrible"), and Assonato ("Sleepy").

"In a way I could have saved myself the trouble," Wilde recalls. "For my command was soon to come to an end—and in a singularly humiliating manner."

Capannette di Pej lay about thirteen miles from the camp, but it was necessary to cover more than twice that distance in order to reach it. The name meant, literally, "The little huts of Pej," and was in fact composed of a group of fifteen barns, outhouses, and sheds high in the hills above the small village of Pej.

Pej lay south-east of San Sebastiano and due south of Varzi. It was in the exact middle of the massif, and the mountains that overhung it were the source of the Staffora, Curone, and many other rivers and streams that ultimately joined the Po. Pej itself was some four thousand feet above sea-level, Capannette di Pej a thousand feet higher. It had two approaches, both following devious, winding routes that had been designed to serve places other than the village. Normally the only people who went to Pej were its own inhabitants.

Nobody else ever passed through, for the two roads just petered out beyond the village. Pej led to nowhere.

They took the most direct route—via a series of paths and goat-tracks across one of the many ridges that shut off Pej from its neighbouring villages. When Wilde and his men approached Pej he expected that they would need to continue on to the *capannette*: he envisaged it as a semi-military encampment taking strategic advantage of the farm buildings and vantage-points. Instead he saw through his binoculars that Capannette di Pej was deserted: the partisan detachments were grouped close to the main village.

As they approached they saw that, apart from the local population, something between three and four hundred partisans were camped in the surrounding fields or were talking in straggling, agitated groups in front of the church. The scene was one of chaos and confusion, with people rushing from group to group, all shouting at the tops of their voices, arguing and gesticulating. As they reached the village square Wilde's partisans broke from their semi-formal column and ran to join the others. Says Wilde, "I felt a surge of anger at this break from discipline—but reminded myself that I was a long way from the parade-ground at Devonport Barracks."

He recognized two of the partisan leaders he had seen at San Sebastiano and went over to them. He asked what was going on, and found that they shared in the general panic and frenzied disorder. Chiri-ci-chi's retreat southward had coincided with a full-scale German reoccupation of San Sebastiano, and there were strong rumours of German successes in other parts of the mountains. The general opinion was that the hitherto ignored rallying-point of Capannette di Pej would be the next enemy target.

There was no suggestion anywhere of making a fight of it. Courage and the will to do battle against the enemy had evaporated, to be replaced by frantic pessimism and self-pitying despair. The only positive suggestion was that the groups should disband, disappear into the mountains, and so live to fight another day. Says Wilde, "I was horrified. I felt certain that the mood of the moment was magnifying the

German success. And as far as an attack on Capannette di Pej was concerned, if the Germans could be drawn so far into the mountains—it would be a gift for the partisans. This was their sort of territory. All manner of ambushes could have been devised to decimate the enemy—and chalk up a great victory."

But Wilde's arrival had come too late to rally the partisans from their morale-shattered defeatism. His one hope, he felt, was by example. He would marshal his own small group, prepare defences, and so shame the others into following him. He went in search of Cesare and found him with Maria, saying farewell to those partisans who were already departing.

Wilde told Cesare what he intended to do. The little man shook his head. "I am sorry. It just isn't possible. If we tried none of the men would join us. As for myself, I don't even want to try. Maria and I will go somewhere for a few weeks —it will be like going on our summer holiday. Then we'll come back and find some good fighting where we can kill more of the pigs. I like fighting against the pigs, and so does Maria. But this disbanding, this going away and coming back when your confidence is restored—that's life. And I don't fight the inevitable. If you do you never win. I am sorry." He shook Wilde's hand in farewell and clicked his heels in mock-Teutonic fashion.

"I am sorry too," said Maria. "I should have liked to fight the Germans and Fascists with you. I am sure we should have killed many together. . . . Perhaps we shall meet again." She took her rosary from inside her shirt and pressed it against Wilde's lips.

He hurried away from them without a word, and went to rally the other members of his detachment. But in the minutes since their arrival many had already gone. From those to whom he was able to speak he received the same reply: respectful, sad, regretful, sometimes ashamed—always firm. In turn they tried to persuade him to join them. It was only a matter of a few weeks, he was assured. They would work on someone's farm. Soon they would start again.

"I was no longer indignant," says Wilde, "but furious.

When I discovered that there was not one single man who would stay and fight I cursed them for a bunch of irresponsible cowards who were only playing at fighting the Germans, and said I was leaving the whole damned bunch of them for ever. I was going to make my way south through the enemy lines and join the British and American forces fighting their way up the peninsula. I felt disgusted with them all."

Up to this moment Wilde did, in fact, have one ally: Eugenio. But when he heard Wilde say he was going south he burst into tears. He assured Wilde that he would go anywhere with him—so long as he could stay in the part of Italy he knew and could fight alongside his own people. But a lengthy trek south . . . He wept bitterly as he shook Wilde's hand and followed a group of his comrades away from the village.

Wilde did not long delay his own departure. He headed north, arguing that it would be quicker to get to one of the main roads than attempt to strike due south through the worst of the mountains. It was a beautiful morning, the brilliant sunshine eased by a light breeze. "Under other circumstances," says Wilde, "I would have enjoyed the hike. But I was bitterly upset. At the first crisis that had cropped up I had failed as a leader. A true commander of men, I told myself, would have had no difficulty in rallying a mere fifty partisans behind him—regardless of the actions of others or the dangers that faced them.

"I felt that it was a sort of punishment for my pride. It had seemed so easy that first day. Now what had happened? One moment I'd been commanding a partisan detachment, with the hope of sufficient success to justify the long period of inactivity in Voghera—now I was just another prisoner of war on the run. So that even if I managed to reach the Allied lines I'd have nothing of value to show for the long months since I'd escaped from the train at Medassino. . . . And so it went on as I worked it out of my system in a great orgy of recrimination."

He had walked for about an hour when a woman passed him on a bicycle, pulled up, dismounted, and waited for him to draw level with her. She guessed he was one of the disbanded partisans, and was curious to know why he was going in the one direction his comrades were avoiding. He dodged the question and merely told her he had been a captain in the partisan army and added—for no good reason—that he was English. She advised him that the Germans were still some distance away down the valley towards San Sebastiano and that the road was temporarily safe. She added that the next village he would pass through was known for its long tongues, and warned him not to speak to anyone except to pass the time of day. With that she pedalled off along the road ahead of him—and Wilde wondered at the length of his own tongue: with his perfect Italian it had been not only unnecessary, but stupid, to reveal his nationality.

Shortly after this encounter Wilde reached a low bridge crossing a small stream. He took off the knapsack he had acquired in camp, which held his binoculars, spare revolver, and a spare shirt he had also obtained while with the partisans. He was bending over the stream, about to wash and drink, when he heard a car approaching from the direction of San Sebastiano. He grabbed at his belongings and hid under the bridge, easing from his trousers the gun he still kept tucked there. As the car went past he saw that it was a black, official-looking saloon, and thought, "The *fascisti*!" The woman had betrayed him. He decided to wait until the occupants of the car realized they had missed him and turned back across the bridge.

But after an hour the car still had not returned, and it seemed as though it was more interested in Capannette di Pej than in himself. He resumed his march along the road, and presently arrived at the village the woman had told him about. Although he was not now inclined to give her story of the villagers much validity he still thought it best to hurry through as fast as he could. He was disturbed, therefore, to see a crowd of people gathered at the outskirts of the village, as though waiting for him. They seemed to know he was *inglese*, and they smiled and clapped their hands and shouted, "Bravo!" At the far end of the village Wilde stopped at a cattle trough brimming with cool, clear water, but as he dipped his face into it he was aware that he was trying to cool off his rage as much as anything else.

A quarter of a mile farther on he heard footsteps pounding the road behind him. He stopped and turned as a breathless young man rushed up. He said he regretted having missed Wilde as he passed through. But there was a partisan leader asleep in the village who, he was sure, would like to meet Wilde. Would he be kind enough to return? "My immediate reaction," says Wilde, "was to refuse: I had no desire to repeat that earlier fiasco. But I agreed, partly because of the young man's tremendous enthusiasm, and partly because, deep down, I suppose I was still hoping to become a partisan."

Wilde was taken to a farmhouse at the edge of the village. The man Wilde had come to see was now awake, preparing to eat a late lunch. He said his name was Gianni; that he was hungry, and so, presumably, was Wilde; and that they would talk when they had eaten. It was a heavy meal, and the red wine flowed generously. Wilde had marched through the previous night, and had spent all of that day on his feet—at Pej and on the road. As Gianni settled down to talk Wilde fell asleep.

Gianni woke him about two hours later, at six o'clock. The partisan leader was tall and slim, bright-eyed and curly-haired, and about twenty-one years of age. "The men who abandoned you at Pej were not real partisans," he assured Wilde. "They are only amateurs who like to pretend they kill the Fascists. . . . But I'll bet on one thing: they left a useful pile of guns and ammunition hidden at Pej."

He suggested that as he had a farm lorry—"borrowed" from one of the more prosperous farms farther down the valley—they should return to Pej and help themselves to whatever equipment was left behind. At first it seemed madness to return to the village which the partisans were so certain was due for an attack—on the other hand it did represent some sort of positive action. So Wilde agreed, and it was not long after their arrival that they uncovered a cache of five *mitras*, several boxes of hand-grenades, and a considerable amount of automatic and revolver ammunition.

They were loading it into the lorry when the same black car that had passed Wilde on the bridge suddenly came round a corner and drove towards them. Wilde dropped the ammunition he was carrying and grabbed for his revolver as four men in civilian clothes jumped out. Only Gianni's shrill cry that they were friends stopped Wilde from opening fire.

Gianni explained that the men, two of them well into middle age, were the organizers of the Voghera resistance movement. They were considered safe by the authorities, which accounted for their having a car and freedom to drive where they liked. Later Wilde gathered they were mixed up in the black market and ran a chain of brothels: activities which made them *personae gratae* to the Fascists. They too had deduced that stocks of equipment would be hidden at Pej, and were anxious to distribute it among the "serious" partisans in the area.

For two hours the six of them searched, and between them uncovered a vast quantity of arms and equipment. As they worked Wilde asked for news of Teresa and Giuseppe, and tried to persuade the four men to get a message to them. But although one of them mentioned briefly that the Bertis were still in the Castello, Wilde was made to understand that the four men were engaged on serious business and had no time to waste on sentimentalities. They divided the spoils proportionately, and without wasting time the saloon car was driven off over the hummocks and boulders.

"Now I will take you to meet some real partisans," said Gianni. "You will see the difference. Yes, you will see." They were going to a village called Castagnola, which lay only about seven miles from San Sebastiano. To get there they would follow the main Curone valley road to within three miles of San Sebastiano, then turn north into the narrower valley of a Curone tributary, the Torbida.

The Castagnola road rose steadily for three miles, shut tightly in on one side by an unbroken mountain ridge, and on the other by a number of individual peaks. As it neared the watershed between the Curone and the Staffora the valley suddenly opened out in the shape of a horse-chestnut leaf. In all, seven valleys of varying sizes fanned out at this point through the crevices of the massif, developing in some cases into sheltered patches of fertile land, often a quarter of a mile wide. Each of the valleys gave access to innumerable mountain hideouts. Castagnola was situated at the point where the seven leaves joined the stalk, as it were, of a major valley. The village was overlooked by an almost vertical cliff; the few paths up it were known only to the local inhabitants.

From a defensive point of view it was perfectly situated. The main valley of the Torbida offered plenty of opportunities for ambush. The seven lesser valleys opened up a wide range of retreat routes. And the paths up and over the cliff-face allowed individuals to be smuggled away from the village quickly and secretly. But Castagnola's greatest virtue was its commanding position in terms of mounting an offensive. Not only was it a perfect holding point when pressure made San Sebastiano indefensible, but it also threatened Varzi. Over the top of the massif it was no more than four miles in a direct line to the centre of the most vital German headquarters in the region after Voghera, even though there was no road and barely any path over the top and down the other side.

As the lorry rolled along Wilde was still not sure that he was doing the right thing. Sitting beside Gianni, a *mitra* between his knees, listening to his description of Castagnola's strategic strength, he still wondered whether he might not be better employed making his way towards the British lines. But they were not far down the road when all doubts were swept from his mind. . . .

A group of women ran from a house to tell them that a Fascist patrol of twenty-four men was raiding a farm about half a mile along a near-by lane. The figure of twenty-four sounded sufficiently precise to be true, but neither Wilde nor Gianni was in the mood to waste time considering the odds.

Gianni backed the lorry behind a wall, and the two men set off down the lane, *mitras* at the ready.

It was not yet completely dark, and Wilde knew they made easy targets for anyone lying in wait. Their attention was concentrated on the ditches bordering the lane, and they were therefore unprepared when a hand-grenade was thrown at them from a tree. But they had time to hurl themselves into a ditch, one on top of the other, before the grenade exploded, sprinkling them with dust and stones. Wilde whispered to Gianni that they had better split up—one on either side of the road. "I swallowed hard," he recalls, "and dashed like mad across the lane. I got there all right, but I was trembling from head to toe. Yet, strangely, I wasn't scared. It was a combination of shock and excitement."

Now started a waiting game. For a few minutes neither side moved. Wilde's attention was then attracted by a sound he could not identify, coming from lower down the lane. He peered cautiously into the middle distance—and it was only from the corner of his eye that he caught sight of a man climbing down from a tree.

He made a perfect target. Wilde took careful aim with his *mitra* and fired a quick burst. The man fell to the ground. Ignoring the danger, Wilde ran over to him. He was not an Italian—as the women had led him to believe—but a German. He was dead. "It was surprising," says Wilde, "how I could tell he was dead just looking at him. And it was surprising, too, how the face of a corpse could carry so much expression—in this case a sort of twisted-lipped sneer. I scurried back to the ditch with all manner of thoughts crowding my mind. I felt I ought to have some pangs of conscience at having killed a man, but I didn't, even though this was the first man I'd directly killed. 'Directly,' because in *Sahib* I'd contributed to the killing of many men. But firing a torpedo towards a target you can't even see is remote and impersonal. This was different; yet my only strong emotion was of being thrilled, of feeling disturbingly exhilarated."

Wilde could still hear the strange sound from down the

lane. He identified it now as something metallic—then glimpsed the source: a German soldier frantically attempting to free the firing mechanism of his sub-machine-gun. Again Wilde aimed and fired. The soldier screamed with pain. At least he was wounded.

It occurred to Wilde that Gianni was curiously silent—then a dozen things seemed to happen at once. A group of enemy soldiers came from among the trees . . . Wilde prepared to take aim . . . a small red object came flying over his head and exploded about fifteen yards in front of him—an Italian grenade from the store at Pej. It fell short of the soldiers, but near enough to send them running for cover. Wilde kept his head down as Gianni continued to hurl grenades into the trees. Then Gianni switched to his *mitra*, and Wilde wriggled behind the protection of a mound of earth and joined in the firing.

From the angle of the fire it appeared that Gianni had moved well down the ditch. Then the firing from the near-by trees and bushes stopped, and was replaced by spasmodic bursts from a range of about five hundred yards—the advance patrol was retreating and was getting covering fire from the rear, Wilde glimpsed two of the soldiers as they ran from their hiding-place some twenty yards away, and fired at them—but without any apparent success.

Suddenly—unnaturally, after all the noise—the woods were silent. Wilde and Gianni waited until they were certain the enemy had gone, then climbed to their feet and complained bitterly to each other about twenty armed men breaking off a fight when the odds were ten to one in their favour. Equally, however, they realized that their moving around must have suggested a much larger force.

They went to the second man Wilde had wounded. He was no longer yelling, but moaning as blood and froth bubbled from his mouth. He was on the point of death, and they made him as comfortable as they could—supporting his head in their hands and washing his face with water from his own water-bottle—until, after five minutes, he died. This time Wilde felt a pang of very real remorse, for the soldier was little more than a boy. "And," says Wilde, "there is a great difference between the sight of a dead man and of a dying one."

But there was no time to be wasted. They took the heavy revolvers from the two corpses, returned to the lorry, and completed their journey to Castagnola.

Gianni was proud of the village, with its two churches and two schoolrooms. It also appeared to have as many inns as private houses. Its normal population was between two and three hundred, but when they arrived there were also several hundred partisans stationed there.

As at Pej, there was an impression of utter confusion and chaos, as partisans moved about in large groups, drinking, arguing, and speculating. But, unlike Pej, the atmosphere here was one of confidence and optimism, of gaiety and self-assurance.

Gianni led Wilde to one of the inns and introduced him to a tall, thin-featured, dark-haired man of about Gianni's own age, known as Primola. His full *nom de guerre*, Wilde gathered, was Primola Rossa ("Red Primrose"). He commanded the entire partisan battalion now in and around the village. Born locally, his real name was Angelo Ansaldi.

The three men ate and drank together, and then a bed was found for Wilde in a near-by house. "A real bed," Wilde recalls. "A bed with a mattress, springs, and beautifully laundered sheets. For a few minutes I lay awake revelling in this unaccustomed luxury. But not for long. From the camp to Capannette di Pej . . . Gianni's farm . . . back to Capannette . . . the skirmish with the Germans . . . on to Castagnola . . . . It had been a long twenty-four hours."

Chapter
EIGHT

Falcon and Red Primrose

WHEN Wilde awoke the events of the previous evening still held a quality of dreamlike unreality. "So much had happened," he recalls, "I found it difficult to believe that any of it had taken place. But it had —my surroundings were proof enough of that, and confirmation came with Gianni inviting me to attend a council of war with Primola Rossa in the dining-room. As I dressed I thought about the two men I had killed, and found I was now quite dispassionate about it: a soldier who had done his duty. No more than that."

In the dining-room Primola unfolded a map, which he spread across the table. He explained that in and around Castagnola he had two hundred and fifty partisans, and, now that Gianni and Wilde had brought in the lorry-load of weapons, each was equipped with a rifle, and there was one *mitra* for every six men. In addition he had three captured mortars, which, by partisan standards, represented a considerable long-range potential.

Primola pointed out to Wilde the local roads and tracks, the location of the enemy forces in the area, and the scenes of the various actions that had taken place that summer. He outlined suggestions for further attacks and asked Wilde for his comments. The Englishman, who hardly considered himself a grand strategist or master tactician, put forward a number of ideas based on plain common sense rather than subtle military reasoning. With some Primola agreed, but when Wilde's proposals clashed with his own dogmatic opinions he was intractable. Finally he asked, "From our base here at Castagnola what should our main objective be?"

"To capture Varzi of course," said Wilde. "You'll have the chance of killing a large number of Germans, but even if you don't, think of the effect on enemy morale. And civilian morale. It would be far more effective than a dozen smaller successes. . . And, looking at the map, I'm not so sure it would be as difficult as it appears."

Primola slammed his hand down on the table. "*Dammi la mano*," he cried, and seized the astonished Wilde by the hand. "You were right, Gianni. This is just the man we want." He went on to explain to Wilde that he and Gianni were planning to leave the battalion at Castagnola for a while to make preparations for just the sort of attack Wilde had suggested: an assault on Varzi. They wanted to regroup certain small and scattered bodies of partisans hiding out in the mountains and carry out some selective recruiting at the same time. They also needed to exchange information and plans with the powerful Communist battalion operating to the north of Varzi.

Before they could leave on these missions, however, they needed to have someone to whom they could entrust the Castagnola command. The purpose of all the questioning, said Primola, was to enable him to judge for himself Wilde's fitness for the job. He had learned of Wilde's escape from the via Cavour and of his brief activities west of San Sebastiano. And Gianni's praise of his part in the previous day's activities had been wildly enthusiastic.

"You have passed the examination," said Primola, smiling. "You are in charge."

"So once again I was a partisan commander," says Wilde. "Only I was absolutely convinced that this time I was involved with the real thing. I was at the heart of the true resistance movement, and if the appointment flattered me I had the self-confidence to believe I could cope with it."

Primola Rossa and Gianni planned to leave that night, now the problem of command had been resolved. They would take fifty men with them to be able to do battle with any enemy patrols they might encounter. As though reading Wilde's mind, Primola assured him that he had no intention of taking the best fifty.

"I smiled at the way my fortunes ebbed and flowed," says Wilde. "From commanding nothing . . . to commanding fifty . . . to commanding two hundred—all within the space of five days. I reflected that even petty officers at gunnery school were not made, broken, and made up again with such speed. Which in turn made me wonder what my shipmates on *Sahib* would think if they were to have seen me at that moment—or whether they'd believe me if I returned home to tell them about it."

Methodically Wilde set about imposing his sense of tidiness and authority on the battalion. He employed the only organizational structure he knew: that of a submarine crew. He introduced two states of preparedness: "Action Stations" and "Diving Stations". "Action Stations" would be the signal for a large-scale operation involving the entire battalion. Between such operations they would be at "Diving Stations" —employed on a planned day-to-day routine. Wilde had the men divided into four squadrons of fifty, each under the command of a lieutenant. The tasks he set them would be rotated, so that each had its fair share of dangers, hard work, and rest. One squadron was sent to patrol the near-by mountain villages; the second guarded the immediate approaches of Castagnola; the third would help the local farmers in exchange for the milk, potatoes, and other food that Wilde proposed commandeering; the fourth rested for the day in the village.

Having worked out his watch-keeping system, and made sure it was thoroughly understood, Wilde next took over the larger of the two village schools as partisan 'barracks'. Its floor space was just about able to provide cramped sleeping-space for those of his men not on guard or at work, or who had not found sleeping accommodation elsewhere in the village—a number of personable young women in Castagnola were willing to provide companionship for lonely partisans. Many such offers were made to Wilde during the period of

James Frederick Wilde, wearing British Army khaki in Italy, 1945

II

A recent photograph of Wilde, his wife, Doreen, and his children Michael and Diane

III The piazza Duomo at Voghera, with market stalls around the cathedral

IV The level-crossing keeper and his wife (*right*) and family, photographed twenty years later in the garden at Medassino through which Wilde escaped

V Clementina Rovati, Adele Goi, Pietro Goi, and Signor Rovati (Frederico's father) outside the Rovati farmhouse at Medassino

VI Pietro's nephew's barn, where Wilde spent several days in hiding

Lindo Ricci ("Falco") outside his home at Bagnaria twenty years after the events told in this book

Teresa and Giuseppe Berti, Voghera, 1963

IX

The entrance to the former Brigata Nera headquarters in the via Cavour, Voghera. Now the offices of the Italian Red Cross

X

The Municipio at Varzi

XI

Don Rino's church at Nivione

XII

The church at Bagnaria, showing the bell that was rung by Falco and Wilde

XIII

One of Wilde's partisans photographed at Varzi in October 1944

XIV

Partisans in Varzi after the liberation of the town

XV The Broken Column, on the roadside from Varzi to Pietra Gavina

his command, but he turned them all down—if only so as not to lose the respect of his men.

The only other regulations he introduced were a ten o'clock curfew and a daily password. The former worked perfectly, as long as he was indulgent towards the occasional collective drinking-party and did not mind whether his more ardent warriors were snuggled in their own or their girl friends' beds at the stroke of ten. The password, however, proved to be a disaster. Neither homecoming partisans nor the guards could be relied upon to remember the word of the day. There was much confusion, with weary patrols losing their tempers and threatening violence, and irate guards fingering their rifles as both sides argued over which was the correct word. Says Wilde, "I quickly learned that one of the first lessons of successful command is to be able to change your mind without thinking that you lose dignity or authority."

Wilde was delighted when, during his first day at Castagnola, a partisan nicknamed "Fulmine" arrived—one of the men Wilde had led towards Serravalle and who had been as bitter and frustrated as Wilde after the disbanding at Pej. On the spot Wilde made him one of his lieutenants.

If Fulmine's coming was a pleasant surprise, Wilde was flabbergasted at the sight of his next recruits. One morning, breakfasting at the inn in the main square, he heard shouts of "*I mongoli! I mongoli!*" He hurried out to discover what the commotion was about, and was confronted by a group of twenty men escorted by partisan guards. Most had high-cheekboned, Slav features, but some did indeed have a slant-eyed Mongolian appearance.

Most had a smattering of Italian, and it transpired that on the Russian front the Germans had recruited troops from among Russian and other prisoners of war. Those who joined up did so because the army offered the opportunity of desertion—and in any case was preferable to the atrocities of the Eastern Front P.O.W. camps. Large numbers of those who had enlisted had been sent to reinforce the German army in Italy, and after a while many had, in fact, succeeded in deserting. This particular group had been roaming the countryside, living off the land and killing any lone Germans they came across. Would they like to join the partisans? Very much—if it meant they would have greater opportunities of killing Germans. Wilde divided them equally among his four squadrons.

There were Hungarians, Czechs, and Poles among the recruits, and two Russians, one of whom, Nicolai, had become strongly attached to an Italian girl from a small farm near Pozzol Groppo. It was only with difficulty that his comrades persuaded him to stay at Castagnola. There was also a Chinese who spoke no Italian at all.

In the days that followed the partisans came to be delighted with their new recruits: not only were the *mongoli* magnificently dedicated fighters, but they had the advantage of being trained soldiers with a high degree of dexterity in mechanical care and maintenance, as well as experience of infantry manœuvring under fire.

A number of Wilde's men had relatives living in or near Varzi, and on a Sunday these people would walk to a point half-way between Varzi and Castagnola to meet their husbands, sons, or brothers. This practice, and the normal comings and goings of the inhabitants of Castagnola, brought Wilde a considerable amount of intelligence about enemy troop movements and about anti-partisan activities in other parts of the Varzi area.

He learned that anti-Fascist feeling was running high at that time among the townsfolk. The German occupation they accepted as though it were an act of God—with resigned fatalism. But persecution by their own people . . . this was a different matter. And the degree of persecution had increased—Wilde's interrogator, Colonel Fiorentini, had moved from Voghera to take command of the combined Axis forces operating out of Varzi. A few days before Wilde's arrival in Castagnola he had taken as hostages, and then executed, two little girls whose brothers were serving with the partisans.

"Somehow," says Wilde, "there was a certain grim humour in the knowledge that Fiorentini was at Varzi."

One of Wilde's lieutenants was twenty-eight-year-old Lindo Ricci, known as Falco. Born locally, he had been a professional soldier—a sergeant in the *carabinieri*—until the Armistice. A giant of a man, he possessed remarkable strength—the person called upon when a lock had to be broken or iron bars needed to be bent apart. He kept his curly brown hair cut short, but wore a full beard and a pair of magnificent, spiky moustaches.

After some days it was Falco who suggested to Wilde that, since things were quiet, they should take a few men and make an expedition of their own: visit the partisans based in the mountains above Pietra Gavina and Zavattarello Valverde. Wilde agreed: he too was now getting restless at the inactivity at Castagnola. So they took sixty men and marched off into the mountains—unaware of the drama towards which they were advancing.

For at Varzi, Fiorentini's spies had informed him of the whereabouts of the Zavattarello group. Two forces of Brigata Nera—one commanded by himself, the other by a junior colonel, Alfieri—set out for the mountains and prepared an ambush.

That night Wilde's squadron marched into it.

They were taken completely by surprise, pinned down from two sides of a right angle. The enemy's firing was heavy, disciplined, and accurate, and although the partisans fired back with rifle and *mitra*, Wilde and Falco knew they were in bad trouble. There was no suggestion of panic, but as the partisans crouched behind rocks and trees firing at the *fascisti*, they were aware that their position was desperately perilous—it was only a matter of time before they would be completely encircled by the much more powerful enemy force.

It was this thought that gave Wilde and Falco a plan for escape. Orders were issued and passed along the line, and fifty of the men ceased firing and quietly withdrew from the battle. Wilde, Falco, and the remainder then speeded up their rate of fire to give the impression that all the partisans were still there—at the same time moving back in an oblique line of retreat so as to tempt the enemy to follow. The Fascists swallowed the bait—each column apparently unaware that the other was also moving. The result: while the few remaining partisans were able to slip away the two groups of Brigata Nera now faced each other in the darkness and were firing from murderously close range. Wilde had no idea for how long the massacre continued before the enemy realized what they were doing, but firing could still be heard half an hour later as the partisans hurried back to Castagnola.

Near disaster had been turned into a formidable victory. While the partisan losses totalled two dead and five wounded, the Fascist casualties must have been enormous. Among them was Colonel Alfieri, who died of the wounds inflicted by his own men.

The incident, not unnaturally, aroused the wrath of Fiorentini and joy in the hearts of the people of Varzi. But jubilation turned to rage and lamentation a few days later when Fiorentini captured three members of the Zavattarello battalion. Without trial or inquiry he had them taken to the spot where Alfieri had been wounded—and shot them. Among Wilde's partisans Giovanni Ballarini, twenty-eight, Stefano Fiori, twenty-two, and Arturo Giannozzi, twenty, acquired the status of martyrs. Says Wilde: "They say events cast long shadows, and these three men were to continue playing their part in the War several months later—implicating me in the process. . . .

"Between patrols and battles I kept the men as busy as I could. I compiled a list of all known Fascist sympathizers among the local farmers and methodically relieved them of their livestock and crops. I also introduced mosquito-sting attacks on the enemy. Whenever a member of the Varzi garrison wandered alone outside the town he could expect to hear a bullet whistle past his ear. I posted the snipers at extreme range because it wasn't the sort of operation that justified hazarding lives, and this meant that the chance of a bullet finding a target was pretty remote. But the messages that came out of Varzi told me that the policy was worthwhile: it gave the enemy garrison the jitters and gave civilian morale a useful boost."

Things were soon to warm up in earnest, but for the moment there was a lull, and this time it was Wilde who suggested a three-day exploratory patrol. Again he was accompanied by Falco, leaving Fulmine in command, but this time they were accompanied by only six partisans. The main object of the patrol was to see if there was any truth in the rumour that major German troop movements north of Voghera were aimed at reinforcing Varzi. It was said that motorized infantry and armoured cars were assembling at Godiasco—the village at the entrance to the Staffora valley to which Serafina had brought Wilde on the train.

They covered the twelve miles to Godiasco in the fast time of five hours. As they travelled together Wilde and Falco became firm friends. Wilde liked the Italian's brash optimism, while Falco never ceased to wonder at the Englishman's complete and natural control of the Italian language. He admired Wilde's mind and liked the way his *capitano* could think up plans to meet any situation, no matter how complicated or desperate. "*Furbu Gems*" he would exclaim, using the expression "Crafty Jim" as a great compliment. From the beginning he was one of the few partisans for whom it seemed natural to call his commander by his Christian name.

"There was no sign of troop activity at Godiasco," says Wilde, "and I felt frustrated at having made a wasted journey. Then Falco, that great extrovert, made a suggestion. There were posters displayed in villages along the Staffora valley offering a large reward for his capture. A number of people in Godiasco knew Falco from the days when he lived in the near-by village of Bagnaria. But he reckoned it was unlikely anyone would recognize him under his huge beard and moustache. His idea was for the two of us to enter Godiasco, call on two or three shopkeepers, and ask for food. To add more spice to the adventure I would pretend to be an Italian partisan, while he would say he was the Englishman everyone now knew was at large somewhere in the area.

"Childish? Stupid? Unnecessarily dangerous? All three, I

suppose, looking back. But I felt in the mood for an adventure of some sort, so I agreed."

One drawback to the scheme was that Falco knew no English, yet had to speak a few words of the language to give his joke some substance. Wilde crammed half a dozen words into him, the most useful of which seemed to be "O.K.", which Falco insisted in thinking of as *oche,* the Italian for "geese".

They left their six men to wait for them and strode off. An hour later they returned with two large baskets filled with a variety of foods, which Wilde had persuaded the shopkeepers to hand over by constant references to the need to impress his gallant English friend. For his part, Falco had kept repeating *oche*, grinning broadly as he did so.

"If, in retrospect, that episode seems infantile," says Wilde, "the one I devised to follow it was equally idiotic. But it must be remembered that we were living keyed to an incredibly high pitch, and any little skylark helped to maintain the necessary tension."

It was evening now, and they were moving quietly along the river-bank opposite Falco's home village of Bagnaria. The *campanile* of the village church rose pink and majestic above the corrugated tiled roofs of the houses. Its bell protruded from an elaborate metal framework. This village they could not enter: even Falco's splendid beard would not serve as sufficient disguise. Further, there was a Fascist guard post on the main road. . . . But Wilde's idea was irresistible.

Again he and Falco left the others behind. They waded the shallow river, advanced close to the first line of houses, set their *mitras* at single shot, and fired, one after the other. Twice the bell rang out with a plangent note. Doors opened and feet scurried up the hill towards the church. Wilde and Falco, feeling for all the world like two small boys enjoying a great success with their catapults, waited long enough to see the guard post disgorge half a dozen *fascisti*, then waded back across the Staffora and continued their journey back to Castagnola.

A guest was awaiting them, a man dressed partly as a

priest and partly in rough mountain clothes. He was in his early thirties, a big man with a round, clean-shaven face and a hand-clasp almost as strong as Falco's. A native of Bagnaria, he was now parish priest of the neighbouring village of Nivione—and, from time to time, a member of one or other of the local partisan bands. His name: Don Rino Cristiani.

Falco was delighted to see him "*Ecco*," he said, pointing first to himself, then to Don Rino: "*Italiano ladro o prete*" ("Italians are either thieves or priests").

Don Rino said he had come to offer his services to Wilde and his partisans, but emphasized that his services were two-fold, "*come prete e come partigiano*" ("as priest and partisan").

They sat and talked until late into the night. Don Rino explained that it had not been an easy decision for a priest to take an active part in warlike activity of this kind. But he felt he had to work in some positive way to help free his country from the anti-Christians. He had written to his local bishop, saying he would be happy to try to combine his duties as a parish priest with his activities as a partisan, but, while he would hate to give up the church he loved so much, he would be prepared to do so if the two pursuits were not considered compatible. He had not had a reply to his letter, and assumed that either someone was turning a blind eye—or they had no spare priest to replace him.

Like Falco and the *mongoli*, Don Rino brought with him some professional military background. Before his appointment as *parroco* of Nivione he had been chaplain of a bersagliere battalion, which, he told Wilde proudly, had been in a number of successful clashes with the British.

Wilde could not resist probing further into what still seemed to him to be conflicting motives: priest and partisan. Don Rino's explanation went like this:

"They say a priest should never get mixed up in politics; should never leave his church—but why not? It depends what one means by politics. If it means deceit and lies, the truncheon and the *mitra*, then a priest should not take part. But if it means getting rid of these things, then why shouldn't a priest play his part? A priest should be the first to bear burdens, defend the innocent, and be prepared to expose himself to danger to help fight the ungodly."

During the first week of August Primola Rossa returned. He brought with him his fifty men—plus a further two hundred. Some were disbanded partisans he had been able to persuade to re-enlist, others were new recruits. This made the total strength at Castagnola close on five hundred. By partisan standards it had become a brigade.

Wilde also learned of the progress of the War—how, by now, the Allies were said to be poised for the invasion of the South of France and, in Italy, were attacking the Gothic Line. "Yet it all seemed strangely remote," says Wilde. "Reality was in the mountains with the partisans."

Wilde told Primola that he would be happy to serve under him in any capacity. To his great surprise—and delight—Primola Rossa would not hear of it. "I can shoot, I can climb, I can lead a charge," he said, "but I cannot command on a big scale as you can. I don't know how to organize. I don't listen to other people's ideas. I'm a hothead. You will stay, and I will serve under you."

Says Wilde: "Having commanded two hundred men, it was not all that difficult to adjust myself to commanding five hundred. The problem had been an initial one: that of getting accustomed to commanding anyone at all! After that it was a matter of degree. In terms of organization the extra men meant dividing the force into two battalions, then subdividing them into squadrons—and finding work for everyone to do."

Two or three days after Primola's return Wilde took him, and a detachment of forty partisans, on an exploratory patrol over the goat-tracks that led across the top of the Bosco Grande. When they reached Castellaro, Wilde split his detachment in two, and sent fifteen of them to raid a farm near Ponte Crenna, on the main Varzi road. The farmer was a Fascist sympathizer and had a son who was a member of Fiorentini's staff. The patrol had successfully stolen the farmer's prize-winning horse and a pair of oxen, and were herding the animals along the road past Nivione, when trouble came.

It was late in the evening, and the men were tired. While nine of the men continued with their booty towards Castellaro the remaining six decided to rest in the sacristy of Don Rino's church: the priest was devoting a few days to the affairs of his parish.

Perhaps there was a spy in the village, or maybe it was just chance, but at four o'clock in the morning a mixed German and Fascist force arrived at the outskirts of Nivione. Led by Fiorentini, the enemy numbered two hundred and eighty men. When they came to the foot of the side-road that climbed to the church they halted—and Fiorentini led a platoon of forty men up the side of the hill towards the church.

The church and presbytery were completely isolated from the rest of the village, which lay a quarter of a mile away. The church had been built on the pinnacle of a little peak covered with oak-trees, flowering almond, and acacia. Its tiny railed terrace looked down through a tracery of boughs and blossoms towards the main road and commanded a perfect view of the gaps in the hills that led to Varzi.

Don Rino was awake and dressed and thinking it would soon be time to ring the angelus—when the calm of the early dawn was suddenly shattered by a burst of machine-gun fire. He ran to the window, and through a chink in the shutters saw a Fascist soldier lying wounded on the footpath that led to the hill. The rest of Fiorentini's platoon were rushing for cover.

The partisan sentry, Sceriffo, had sighted the enemy as they climbed the hill. At the sound of the *mitra* burst the five remaining partisans hurried from the church and spread out in the bushes and trees. Sceriffo crawled from one to the other of them, and said that, as he was wearing what might pass at a distance for a German uniform, he had the best chance of getting past the enemy and carrying news of the attack to Wilde. It was agreed, and he slipped away down the hill, firing a random burst as he went.

The five partisans held their fire as Fiorentini reformed his troops and ordered them to advance. They reached a point where they could no longer be seen by the main force below —and it was then that the partisans opened fire. The enemy were still devoting their attention to the area from which Sceriffo had fired . . . and found themselves being attacked from two other directions. As had happened so often in the past, the imagination of the ambushed could see an enemy behind every twig and leaf. The partisans emphasized this impression by darting from bush to bush and tree to tree, firing short bursts as they went. In a few minutes the enemy was no longer a strong punitive force, but a beleaguered salient.

They were now grouped close to the presbytery, and Don Rino could watch their disordered movements, observe the fear on their faces, and hear their orders, counter-orders, and exaggerated appraisals of the situation.

"We're bottled up," a white-faced Fiorentini kept repeating—even when the partisan fire died away as the five men retreated down the hill. For a full twenty minutes the platoon crouched in silent fear. A sergeant broke the spell, addressing the young officer under whose command the platoon normally operated. "Well, captain, what should we do?"

The captain did not reply, but Fiorentini said, "Captain, climb the church tower and tell me what you can see."

On hands and knees the captain crawled towards the church tower. Some minutes later Don Rino saw him clinging unhappily to the eaves of the square *campanile*, a foot wedged in one of the four round-topped archways through which the bells gazed out across the countryside. But he could see nothing and hear nothing, for by now the partisans were half a mile away, retreating along the line of woods that ran parallel to the main road towards Castellaro, from which they hoped Wilde and Primola would be coming.

It was not long before they met them, following the path through the woods known only to the partisans. As soon as Sceriffo had arrived to report the attack Wilde sent a man to Castagnola to take the news to Falco, whom he had left in charge there. He left behind at Castellaro the nine men who had returned during the night with the horse and cattle, so with Primola and the five partisans he met on the road his force numbered thirty-one. By partisan standards the odds were not unusually high.

Three of Fiorentini's platoon had been killed, and four wounded, before the partisans withdrew. And as the hillside continued to show no sign of activity, Fiorentini sent a messenger to the main force below—it had remained inactive, apparently happy to take no part in the fighting—with orders for a further hundred men to be sent up. The remainder he deployed, some to continue to guard the main road, the others to cover the other road that led from the church—the road to Nivione village.

Wilde and Primola were advancing as fast as they were able. Wilde sent Primola and three others to a position from which they could cut off any retreat from the church down the road to the main highway. He knew he did not have time to make a long circuit to ambush the other road—he could only hope the enemy would return by the road by which they had come.

By this time Fiorentini had entered the church and spoken to Don Rino. He asked a number of searching questions, which the priest was able to evade and parry without actually having to tell a lie. He was wondering for how long he could continue to ward off the colonel, when there was another burst of *mitra* fire. It was Wilde himself, who had approached to within twenty yards. As Don Rino looked out he could see one man lying dead. A few seconds later another soldier fell across the terrace of the church, shot through the throat. And a German sergeant, racing across to the safety of the presbytery, caught a spray of machine-gun bullets across both calves. The priest dragged him in and set to work washing and bandaging his wounds.

For a while there was heavy firing on both sides, although Fiorentini's men had little idea of where their targets lay. Both sides now had good cover, and although a great deal of ammunition was used, there were no further casualties. Primola cursed himself for not having brought a mortar, and both he and Wilde were aware that theirs was now a holding action: to keep the enemy pinned down until the brigade arrived from Castagnola.

But Fiorentini had no intention of remaining where he was. He must have guessed that the route to the main road might be guarded, for he gave orders for his detachment to take the other path—the one to the village. He moved his men round to the far side of the hill and down to Nivione, leaving a strong rearguard.

It was a well-planned and skilfully executed manœuvre. Primola's chance came when the rearguard itself withdrew: before it reached the bottom of the hill it had lost six men. The partisans did not follow, for they could now see the troops Fiorentini had posted there.

Wilde and Primola were jubilant. Although the action had not been as conclusive as they would have liked, at least they had inflicted a number of casualties at no cost at all to themselves. And there was the knowledge of the effect the success of this sort of action must have on enemy morale. But their satisfaction was short-lived. . . .

As they looked down towards Nivione they saw a fire . . . another . . . then another. In a matter of minutes the village was ablaze: houses, farm buildings, and crops. With Don Rino the partisans raced down the hill—just as the brigade from Castagnola arrived. Soon they were all hard at work, rescuing women and children, salvaging furniture, releasing trapped animals, and attempting—unsuccessfully—to fight the flames.

Within an hour almost the entire village was gutted. No one was killed, but the partisans realized that victory had been turned into sour defeat. They were grateful for only one thing: that Fiorentini had not had the sense to set an ambush for the partisans as they descended the hill.

Wilde, Primola Rossa, and Don Rino began organizing the rehabilitation of the villagers. Says Wilde: "There could be no doubt as to our next move. We needed a resounding, indisputable victory—and an early one at that. It was not only a case of revenge being sweet, but an immediate counterblow was vital in terms of morale. And a high morale was our most precious asset if we were to continue working for a full-scale attack on Varzi."

Chapter
NINE

Catholics and Communists

THERE was a great deal of activity during the next few days. Units of Fiorentini's German armoured-car squadron, which for some reason had not accompanied the force he brought to Nivione, were reliably reported to be scouring the entire area south and west of Varzi. Wilde increased his patrols, telling them to report back by messenger at the first sign or news of the enemy. He bitterly regretted that he had no satisfactory system of long-distance communication, and that the enemy soldiers they had killed had no walkie-talkie apparatus.

On the second day after the burning of Nivione he decided to leave Primola Rossa in charge at Castagnola while he visited Falco, whom he had sent on patrol with ten men near Varzi. He had not been with them long when, during a brief rest period, a look-out reported that two armoured cars were approaching from some distance along the road. Falco looked inquiringly at Wilde, but the Englishman told him that since he was the officer in charge of the patrol it would only be proper for him to set the ambush.

The place at which they had halted was ideally suited to the purpose. This was not good fortune—Wilde had laid down that patrols should rest only at positions of advantage, so that they could never be taken by surprise and would always be able to take the offensive.

They were at the bottom of a narrow ravine. On one side the road to it wound downward steeply and openly—not shut in by rocks and trees or difficult contours. On the other side of the ravine the road wound upward equally steeply, and with as many bumps and hairpin bends—but it was hemmed in on both sides by high rockfaces. The two roads met at what in the rainy season was the ford of a fast-running stream. But the summer drought had long since removed the last drop of water. What remained to link the two roads was a bed of close-packed, irregularly sized rocks which would reduce to well below walking pace the speed of even the most wildly irresponsible armoured-car driver.

So what the armoured cars would have to do was come down the hemmed-in road, cautiously cross the river-bed, then make their way up the road where Wilde and his partisans were now waiting.

Just where the river-bed gave way to this road there stood a huge finger of rock, some twelve feet high by eight broad. Behind this Falco hid nine members of the patrol, as well as himself and Wilde, sending the remaining man to join the look-out at his post high up on the other side of the ford. The plan was straightforward.

The steepness of the road down which the armoured cars were approaching was such that they would be unable to keep to a tight nose-to-tail formation. This, Falco argued, was a mixed blessing, for it would improve his chances of dealing with the first, but would give the second a greater opportunity for reversing out of trouble. (It did not occur to Falco that any German armoured-car commander would want to do anything but retreat when he attacked them!) As soon as the wheels of the leading car were among the uneven rocks of the river-bed the two men on the other side of the ford would open rapid fire with their *mitras*. This would result in the turret of the armoured car being swung in their direction—for the vehicles were solid and formidably equipped and, but for the absence of caterpillar tracks, more like light tanks.

The moment the turret swung away from them the men behind the rock would rush out to throw Molotov cocktails—petrol bombs fashioned from empty wine- and beer-bottles—through the car's front vizor and under its wheels. Four men would be enough for this, Falco decided: more would only get in each other's way. The remainder would put up a barrage to keep the second car at bay if it appeared to be approaching the ford too quickly.

Wilde told Falco that he would be one of the bomb-throwers. For a moment the big man's face registered surprise: he could not understand why Wilde had found it necessary to make such a statement—as commander it was his privilege to take part in the major part of the action, because it meant a more probable chance of killing Germans.

They did not have long to wait. There was a rumbling and a crash of gears as the first car came into view. It negotiated the final bend, rolled slowly towards the dried-up river-bed, then stopped a few yards short of the first of the rock formations. It was low and broad, still camouflaged in the browns and yellows of the North African desert. A red-and-white pennant hung limply from its wireless aerial. With the exception of its vizor all its ports were closed.

Says Wilde: "I tried to imagine how unbearably hot it must have been inside. I could feel the claustrophobia I would experience if I were in there—and this made me wonder, irrelevantly, how some people could see a similarity between tanks and submarines."

Falco whispered, "I wonder if it's going to wait for the second one before crossing the ford."

Wilde looked at his colleague and said he'd welcome it, even though it would add considerably to the dangers of the operation.

The car slammed into gear. Cautiously it edged its way among the grey and white boulders—and the two *mitras* opened up from high on the slope.

Wilde recalls: "Things seemed to happen without me having time to think—except that as I ran from cover it flashed through my mind that the two partisans over the river might not remember to fire sufficiently wide off target. And I remember feeling that it would be bloody daft to be shot by one of my own side. . . . I was shoulder to shoulder with Falco, and my senses recorded odd snippets of detail—

the crunch of the armoured car's wheels over the rocks . . . the smell of the overheated engine. . . .

"I shoved my cocktail down the vizor, and Falco's followed a fraction of a second later. Then the two of us backed away. As we did so the two partisans who had followed us lobbed their bombs under the front and rear axles.

"We were barely a couple of yards away when the car exploded. For about the time it takes to wink an eye there seemed to be noise, *then* the sight of the explosion as we flung ourselves flat on the bed of the river. It seemed literally to rain lumps of rock and metal. I felt something hot and sharp land on the small of my back. I swung round, more surprised than hurt.

"There wasn't much left of the armoured car, but I remember being disappointed that it was there at all. Anyway, it had certainly been completely destroyed. What remained was a twisted chassis to which one front and one rear wheel were still attached—although at crazy angles. The top of the car had been blown wide open, and a plume of oily black smoke was coming from it. Around the car was a cloud of rock and metal dust. Oddly, although the dashboard, steering-wheel, and steering-column had been blown far away from the car, they were still a complete unit.

"A German soldier was stretched, charred in the oily flames, across the car's bonnet. Another body had been blown right over my head. The uniform had the insignia of an officer, and he was still clutching his Luger—but he had been decapitated."

The other partisans came running up, helped Wilde and Falco to their feet, and congratulated them on their victory. But their whoops of joy were silenced by the sight of Frederico, who had taken care of the rear axle, lying dead. He had been hit by a cannon shell—and this made Wilde and Falco realize that the second armoured car must have put in a brief appearance. It could only have been a shell from this second car that had hit Frederico. The partisans across the river confirmed this: the second car had rounded the final bend of the road just as the four men rushed to the attack. Its shells had whistled past them as they dashed over the river-bed—but in their excitement they had been deaf and blind to everything except the job in hand. Frederico had been hit just as he began his retreat. Despite the concentrated fire of the partisans it had seemed that the armoured car would soon wipe out the other three bomb-throwers. But the explosion inside the leading car . . . the sudden gush of flame and shower of metal . . . and the second car turned round and hurried back along the road it had come from.

"Out of fear," said Falco.

"For reinforcements," said Wilde.

In either event there was no point in their remaining. They hurriedly buried Frederico and the two Germans by piling stones some three feet high over their heaped-up bodies. They looked for other corpses in the car, and although they were certain that a crew numbered four, they were unable to find even a limb of the others.

Falco stood in silence for a moment beside the grave, then murmured a short Latin prayer and crossed himself reverently. Seconds later he turned to grin at Wilde, repeating the joke he had made at Castagnola. "*Ladro*", he said, gesturing towards the wrecked car 'stolen' from Fiorentini. "And *prete*" —pointing to the grave over which he had prayed.

Then they headed back to camp. From the top of the first hill they looked back at the scene of their ambush. The twisted, blackened vehicle had the appearance of a special symbol: a token of partisan determination. The thought came to Wilde that Fiorentini might think that it would be bad for morale if the wreckage were left there—even though the road was seldom used—and decided to post a sniper at a long-range position.

"I was feeling stiff and sore by now," says Wilde. "The fragment of metal that had hit me in the back had fortunately been pretty well spent, and although my shirt was torn and bloodstained the gash in my back was only a deep scratch. I think I was suffering more from the bruises—plus the tension and excitement of the past few days. Within five minutes of arriving back at Castagnola I was fast asleep."

Excitement—and sadness. And there was much sadness during the days following the burning of Nivione; the grief only partially eased by Wilde and Falco's success against the armoured car. Some inhabitants of the village had fled, first to take refuge in the woods and fields, later to the homes of relatives and friends in the neighbourhood. With the exception of a few men who, like the extrovert Falco, regarded the business of killing Germans as something in the nature of a splendid game, the partisans searched for the enemy with sorrow in their hearts as well as the burning desire for revenge.

Don Rino's presbytery was now being used as the partisans' advance headquarters. Day and night, at all hours of the clock, it was a calling place for partisans travelling to and fro on patrol, needing something to eat and drink and somewhere to gather and leave information. The day after the incident of the armoured car Wilde and Primola returned to Nivione to look over partisan activities there. Wilde had a hunch that the *fascisti* would not resist returning there in the near future, and he was anxious to prepare a suitable reception.

No sooner had they arrived than they were greeted with the news that a small detachment (it turned out to be thirty men) was on its way to join them from the Communist partisan group which operated under the name of the Brigata Arzani. This brigade was currently operating in the upper reaches of the rivers Curone and Borbera, mostly to the west of Capannette di Pej, providing a link with the area that had formerly come under the command of Chiri-ci-chi. Commanding the brigade was Franco Anselmi, whose *nom de guerre* was Marco. Even though his own forces were hard pressed from the west, he had heard of the brave actions that had been carried out south of Varzi, and also of the burning of Nivione. The token force he was sending came as a gesture of "fraternal friendship".

When they arrived the Communists were accommodated temporarily in the presbytery. There was no embarrassment or ill-will between themselves and Don Rino. It was argued that no matter how much the Church and the Communists may have disagreed before the War—and would doubtless disagree again when the fighting was over—at the moment they were united (at least with Don Rino) against a common enemy.

It began to rain. Hour after hour it poured down with fierce intensity, bringing all movement to a halt. As they waited for a break in the weather the Communists and Wilde's own partisans gossiped and drank, exchanging elaborate toasts and dramatic oaths of loyalty. "*Moriemo assieme, se sara necessario, ma mon passerano*" ("We will die together, if necessary, but they shall not pass") was the Verdun-like proclamation of the leading Communist. Eventually the rain did cease, and the men returned to their guard posts and patrol areas.

Late on the night of August 11th Wilde set out on his rounds, distributing rations of precious cigarettes at the guard posts. Although it was no longer raining, the sky was still overcast and unrelieved by even a solitary star. As he returned to the presbytery he thought that it was an ideal night for an enemy attack.

He was right.

In the early hours of the following morning some two hundred *fascisti*, commanded by Fiorentini's 'hyena', Pastorelli, took advantage of the darkness and the blanketing sound of water coursing down the rivers and along the streams. By walking ankle-deep in the river Lella they avoided the partisan outposts, and turned west before Nivione along a little-used path that led to a ruined farmhouse, the Casa Bressafame. This was the highest building for several miles, higher even than the Nivione church—from which it was only half a mile distant—higher by some five hundred feet. When they reached the farmhouse the Fascists broke ranks and settled down in silence to await the dawn.

At the same time another enemy force, also two hundred strong, left Bagnaria, heading eastward. The plan was straightforward. Pastorelli reckoned that news of his detachment's whereabouts would finally reach the partisans. They would attack him, and he would either defeat them or contain them. In the latter event it would not be long before the other Fascist force arrived and closed the trap. Further, he was strategically placed for a rapid withdrawal to the heavily guarded plains surrounding Varzi. At the very worst he would take sufficient prisoners to make both excellent propaganda and work for the firing-squad.

A first-class plan—except for one thing: the remarkable mobility of the partisans over rough terrain, coupled with their extraordinary powers of recovery after a setback. Pastorelli's scheme was excellent—if he were granted sufficient time.

Pastorelli and his force were spotted far earlier than he had anticipated. A messenger sped with the news to the presbytery. Although no one knew of the supporting force coming from Bagnaria, the partisans acted speedily from force of habit. As soon as they were mustered, Wilde marched them to the summit of Mount Dego, which overhung the Casa Bressafame. A partisan who had spent all his life in the area acted as a guide, and by cutting straight across ground which even seasoned local villagers would have thought impossible to cross the partisans reached the summit an hour after leaving Nivione.

Soon it would be daylight, and Wilde had little time to prepare an elaborate scheme. His force totalled fifty men, and he deployed them in defensive formation along the slopes of the mountain, running diagonally downward towards Bressafame. He spaced them twenty yards apart, each man well hidden in the bushes. He ordered them to keep as still and silent as they could, and told them that in no circumstances must they open fire until he gave the signal. In the meantime they should hold themselves "*pronti a scattare al mio cenno*" ("ready to jerk at his nod").

First light came at four-thirty. Wilde ordered the four men he had set at the highest point of the diagonal to open spasmodic rifle fire on the Casa Bressafame. They did so, and it was not long before Pastorelli sent the bulk of his troops marching up the slopes above the farmhouse—although he himself decided to remain at the Casa.

The *fascisti* moved slowly and carefully, occasionally firing random rifle-shots and machine-gun bursts as they went. The four partisans fired back, but on Wilde's orders they did so at long intervals, to give the impression that they were conserving their ammunition. To Don Rino, watching and listening from the courtyard of his little church, and not knowing Wilde's plan, the heavy enemy firing and the light, sporadic partisan response was puzzling. Yet he was not too worried: he knew his partisan comrades would not accept defeat without a bitter fight. Soon after six o'clock he decided he ought to make his own contribution to the battle. So he celebrated Holy Mass there and then, dedicating it to the group of partisans high above him in the hills. His devotions finished, he climbed his square *campanile* for a better view.

By now the Fascists had advanced high up the mountain. For minutes on end there would be no firing at all. Then came another burst from the enemy, followed by a few shots from the mountain peak. Often the *fascisti* were only a few yards away from hidden partisans, and some of Wilde's men were now much lower down the slope than the rearmost Fascists. It was a perfect trap—and suddenly it was sprung.

Wilde gave his signal—a burst of *mitra* fire which cut down four of the enemy—and the partisans attacked.

Grenades were hurled from the bushes. More men fell, and the two young officers leading the advance could do nothing to stem the confusion or bring order from the chaos. Even as he fired his opening burst Wilde realized he could turn surprise into a rout. Jumping up from behind his hiding-place, he yelled, "*Partigiani all' assalto!*" The partisans charged, firing as fast as they were able. The Fascists fled.

Thirty were killed in the initial rush, and more fell as they stumbled down the hill. The difficulty of the terrain, and the accurate covering fire that now came from the farmhouse, prevented the partisans from turning the retreat into a massacre. But it had been a good day's work for all that.

They hastened back to Nivione. Don Rino came out to meet them: a happy, weary crowd of men, soaked with sweat, their clothes torn and dirty. But their eyes were proud, and they ate their bread and drank their wine in the manner of victors.

They told and retold their own versions of the battle of Dego, as it came to be called, and then went on to recount tales of other victories—some great, some small. Wilde's own contribution to these was the story of one of his mosquito attacks on the enemy guard around Varzi. He had discovered a detachment of enemy troops lying completely under cover on the slope of a hill. They were well hidden—except that they did not realize that the sun was glinting on their helmets, to create a score of tiny marker-beacons. The fun of shooting at them, said Wilde, was almost matched by observing through his binoculars the perplexed expressions on their faces as they retreated.

For all the partisans the war against the Germans and Italian Fascists meant involving their families in great hardship and exposing them to terrible dangers. The soil on the local farms was so barren and unyielding that the absence of an able-bodied man meant that a tremendous extra burden of toil was placed on those left behind, as they tried to scratch some sort of existence from their fields. And there was always the chance that the absence of a son or a husband would be noted by the *fascisti*, who would assume he had joined the partisans. Or there could be a traitor in the village. Either way, it meant, at the best, the burning of buildings and crops and the slaughter of cattle; at the worst, the death of the absent man's family.

Among the partisans themselves there was a sharp division of attitude towards fighting the enemy. For many of them, like Falco, it was an exciting and enjoyable activity—somewhat comparable to a day's hunting. For others hatred and the desire for revenge were the dominating factors. And there were those motivated by a sense of duty: volunteers in a war against brutality and evil.

One of the partisans at Castagnola had been concerned in an exchange of prisoners—one partisan for one German—that had taken place shortly before Wilde arrived from Capannette di Pej. He had been interrogated by the Germans in their own particular manner, and when he arrived back among his comrades he had torn gums to show where teeth had been removed without anæsthetic, and crippled fingers from which the nails had been torn in the same manner. Further, the inside of one forearm was badly burned as a result of lighted cigarettes being placed on it. Paradoxically, however, he was one of the less vocal when it came to expressing hatred of the enemy, and seemed unmoved when, a few days after the battle of Dego, a patrol brought in a handful of German prisoners.

Wilde assigned them to various labouring jobs, and one of them, who could speak Italian, started a conversation with the ex-prisoner. Unemotionally the man showed his gums, his fingers, and his forearms, and told the German that this was the work of his comrades—the sort of thing no partisan would ever stoop to. The German interrupted him and arrogantly assured the partisan that his torturers could not have been German: his countrymen would never commit atrocities. He had been maltreated by the Brigata Nera, and was so ashamed of his own countrymen that he put the blame on the Germans.

They were in the bakery at the time, and before anyone could stop him the little partisan opened an oven, took from it a huge handful of still-soft dough, and slammed it into the face of the German, holding it there as the man screamed and staggered backward. "If I'm prepared to have another sore hand you can have a hot mouth," he said—and walked away. For days afterwards the German suffered dreadfully from his burned face, mouth, and gums, but the little partisan never mentioned his skinless hand and would not accept treatment for it. Nor did he ever again refer to the incident.

"And so the pattern continued," says Wilde. "There were numerous small clashes and incidents. We were always on the winning side—if for no other reason than that we were tying up a large garrison in Varzi.

"By September I learned that the Allies had crossed the Metauro and that they were attacking towards Bologna. I still retained my extremely valuable capacity for closing my mind to anything but the events of my day-to-day existence. Had it been otherwise my state of mind would at times have been very depressed—hidden away in the Italian mountains, a stranger in a strange land, with no idea of when I would see my home and loved ones again, if at all. Naturally, there were times when I did think of them—particularly in the small hours, gazing upwards at the stars and wondering, fancifully, whether they too might be looking at that very same star at that very same moment. But when my thoughts became too pessimistic and depressing I shut them from my mind."

Chapter
TEN

The Battle of Varzi: First Day

A LANDMARK of the next few weeks was a meeting between Wilde and the two principal Communist partisan leaders in the area. Pressure to the north of Varzi had eased temporarily, and he received a message that the *Comandante* and the *Commissario* of the Third Lombardia Division were crossing into his territory. Together with Don Rino and Primola Rossa he met them at Nivione, on the terrace of the church. Neither the Communists nor the priest were in any way embarrassed by the encounter.

The *Comandante* was the military leader, the *Commissario* the organizing and administrative brain and the political head. The former was a short, white-faced, frail man with straight black hair, known as Americano. He was very conscious of his rank, and not prepared to be on the informal footing with his escort of rankers as was Wilde. When Primola Rossa introduced the *Comandante* to Wilde he stressed that Americano was not a countryman from the north, but a townsman from Tuscany. He said this with straight-faced gravity, and, knowing Primola's general contempt for townsmen, Wilde realized for the first time that the austere, dogmatic Rossa had some sense of humour. The *Commissario*, Piero, was another townsman—a journalist from Milan, tall, well built, smartly dressed, and with his fair hair cropped short. . . . His first remark was to comment on Wilde's well-shaven cheeks, saying that he had a theory that daily shaving indicated a tidy, alert mind. Wilde immediately felt better disposed towards Piero than towards Americano—although in theory, because of their respective rôles, the *Comandante* should have been the more interesting and powerful personality.

It transpired that earlier in the year Americano and his men had been operating south of Varzi. While doing so they had got their hands on between five hundred and six hundred complete sets of motor-car and lorry tyres. Americano had hidden them away just to the south of Varzi's main bridge over the Staffora—in a position so close to enemy headquarters as to make it utterly free from suspicion. The tyres were buried in a vast hole his men had dug beside the river and covered with a mound of stones. Americano was very proud of his cache and explained that its purpose was to provide funds for the Communist revolution that would inevitably follow the ultimate victory.

Wilde attempted to persuade Americano to part with a fraction of his hoard, knowing it would fetch a great deal of money in the Voghera black market. "The Communists deserve a successful uprising in the valleys," said Wilde diplomatically, "but if we could sell just a fraction of the tyres now both our commands would be almost self-supporting. My men are short of money, and yours must be, too. You know how it is when men are worried about their families. They are all poor, living penniless on neglected farms. I don't want the money for myself—but my men and their families have a desperate need for it." He did not expect to persuade the Communist commander, nor did he.

They made plans for future co-operation, and in particular they discussed the importance of Varzi. They parted on friendly enough terms, both sides knowing that a binding sense of honour would guarantee that the hidden store of tyres would remain untouched by Wilde or his men.

During their discussions the Communists had noticed how much Don Rino had contributed to the conversation. They had heard of the partisan priest, but had not known just how much they could rely on the stories circulated about him.

Now they agreed that he was a genuine and active anti-Fascist, and felt that he could be of enormous use to them, if only because of the freedom of movement he enjoyed in and out of Varzi. Before they left for Zavattarello they struck a bargain with him. On his side he would agree to visit them at intervals, supply them with information, and carry messages. For their part they would appoint him *cappellano* ("chaplain") of the Third Lombardia Division and permit him to carry out his priestly duties among their partisans.

A week later Don Rino visited them at Zavattarello, and was presented with an impressive, typewritten document carrying the division's official stamp—the head of Garibaldi set inside a red star. The document, dated September 30th, 1944, was signed by Americano and Piero and headed "The Body of Volunteers for Liberty, Adherents to the Committee of National Liberation, Order of the Garibaldi Assault Brigade, Third Lombardia Division" and ran:

1. We have asked the priest Don Rino, in his capacity as military chaplain, to supply religious and spiritual assistance to the Garibaldini of the Third Lombardia Division, and we are grateful for his prompt and generous affirmative response.
2. We have guaranteed him complete and unconditional freedom and the proper support in the carrying out of his priestly ministrations.
3. We do not ask of him any participation in political propaganda, in order to leave him the fullest liberty, as in the case of every other Garibaldino, to bear witness to the judgment of the Catholic faith, its actions and ideas.
4. We have given him the fullest liberty to retire to a private life if ever any of the above written items of declaration are contravened, or if the actions of the Garibaldi Brigade should in any way diminish his priestly dignity, or else if the religious authorities in a judgment beyond his control should order him to do so.

Don Rino agreed with Wilde that it was a masterly document. His friendship with Americano and Piero prospered—for about a month. Then he discovered that Americano had ordered the execution of a party of German prisoners. On his next meeting with the two Communists he told them that when proper law and order were restored he would report that act of inhumanity—just as he would report the behaviour of Fiorentini. The Communist leader smiled and put an arm round his shoulder. "Let us worry about what happens later when the time comes. Right now there's a war on."

By early October Wilde sensed that, despite minor successes in the past weeks, enthusiasm at Castagnola was in decline. Since the incident of the armoured car and the battles of Nivione and Dego, the enemy forces had kept close to Varzi. The partisans were short of action—and this meant they had more and more time in which to compare their own bored inactivity with the work they could be doing on their farms. Again Wilde bitterly regretted Americano's refusal to part with some of his tyres: the money would have alleviated a great deal of unrest as well as poverty. But he kept to his policy of not attempting to hold any man who wished to return home, and made certain his lieutenants reflected this attitude. In the case of the intense Rossa and the fiery Falco it was not the easiest point of view to put across.

Further, there had been renewed enemy pressure on Capannette di Pej from both west and east. It seemed to Wilde that this behind-the-lines regroupment area had assumed too great an importance in the minds of both the partisans and the enemy. On the other hand, some of the Varzi garrison had been sent to assist in the operations around Pej, which meant that the town's garrison had been weakened. In terms of his hopes for an attack on the town Wilde was therefore not displeased with this development. By the same token he was not too unhappy when he lost the Communists of the Brigata Arzani, who felt they would rather be fighting at Pej than waiting outside Varzi—the more partisans at Pej, the greater the enemy force that would be tied up there.

Wilde's force had now dwindled to about three hundred men. Since his association with Americano and Piero he had adopted the partisan practice of giving each force a specific name, and his now had the title of the Aliotta Division. It was equivalent to, but smaller than, Americano's Lombardia Division. Both, he learned, were part of the Garibaldi Assault Brigade—although the location of Brigade headquarters and the name of its commander were mysteries to him. The one thing Wilde was not prepared to do with such a relatively small force was to divide it into ten battalions, irrespective of their size, as did other partisan commanders. Instead he retained the system of four lieutenants, each in charge of sixty men. The one concession he made was to rename them battalions instead of squadrons. Primola Rossa remained second in command, and also commanded a special mobile battalion, also approximately sixty strong, drawn from men who were normally part of the headquarters force at Castagnola.

In assembling information to help him plan an attack on Varzi Wilde drew on a number of sources. None approached in volume or value that which came from a certain Don Tino. It was confusing that the curate of Varzi had a name so similar to that of the priest at Nivione—particularly since so much of Don Tino's information came to him via Don Rino. In appearance, however, the two men were quite dissimilar. While Don Rino was big and rugged like Falco, the priest from Varzi was short and baby-faced, kindly and gentle. He felt he could best help fight the Fascists by remaining in the town, conforming to the various rules and regulations—at the same time giving what strength he could to both the people of his parish and the political and military prisoners in the Castello. But this did not stop him from leaving the town from time to time, evading the series of road blocks and sentry posts, and hurrying to Nivione with news and advice.

On October 14th Wilde received vital news from Don Tino: the following day there was to be a movement of troops from Varzi to Voghera.

Wilde and his lieutenants were elated. Said Primola: "What an ambush we can make! What a reception we'll give them. It will be costly, but worth it, especially since there's been nothing much happening for so long."

Wilde shook his head. To him the news meant much more. With part of the Varzi garrison, including the remaining armoured cars, operating around Capannette di Pej, the movement of troops meant that enemy strength in the town would now be at its lowest since before he arrived at Castagnola at the end of July. This suggested more than an ambush.

Wilde proposed attacking Varzi.

It would not only be the greatest victory they had achieved so far, but would cut a major line of enemy communications, and would reverberate around the entire province to give anti-Fascist morale a boost unequalled by any previous partisan success.

During the morning of the troop movement Wilde completed his plans. Equipment was checked and re-checked and ammunition distributed. Wilde proposed leading four battalions to the attack. The fifth would take the one remaining mortar and act as strategic reserve. The command of this force went to a reluctant Falco, who was furious not to be in the thick of the fighting. But Wilde argued that on a venture of this kind it was essential that his reserve—on whom the final outcome might well rest—should be commanded by one of his best men. Falco accepted the assignment on the promise that he would be called into the fight as soon as possible. Falco had one final task. As well as acting as the reserve his force would, paradoxically, go in ahead of the main body—as far as the outskirts of the town. There they would be responsible for cutting all telephone lines and for severing rail communications between Varzi and Voghera by blowing up a crossing.

"Morale was high," says Wilde, "and the sensation of excitement in Castagnola was almost a physical thing. There was no feeling of caution or doubt: this was what we had been waiting three months for. Early on the morning of October 15th we marched out."

Wilde led his partisans quickly and quietly through Dego village—on the other side of the mountain from the spot where he had won his victory two months earlier—before turning eastward past the hamlet of Casa Bertella. To their delight they were joined there by Don Rino. It was still dark when they waded the shallow waters of the Staffora, far enough west of the Varzi bridge to escape detection by the sentries. This brought them to one extreme end of the town, and meant that they would be doing all their fighting in one direction. They crouched down in the hollow of a field that ran from the back of the railway station to the river, and awaited Wilde's signal.

"In the quiet of the dawn every sound and movement seemed curiously magnified," Wilde recalls. "I could hear muffled curses around me as someone dislodged a stone and a man knocked his *mitra* against his ankle . . . I looked at my watch. It was zero hour. In another minute Falco would be late with his blowing up of the track. But there was no question of turning back. . . . Then I heard a dull explosion in the distance and jumped to my feet. I gave a yell that was so loud I almost frightened myself.

"The battalions followed me, and within seconds we were across the narrow shunting-yard and through the goods depot to the streets of the town. At first the only sounds were our own footsteps and voices, for most of us were still yelling our heads off. The first shots came from somewhere ahead of us in the centre of the town, and I guessed they were probably from sentries giving the alarm. My own men did not fire back since I'd ordered them not to waste bullets or grenades until they could see someone or something to shoot at."

As planned, the men fanned out when they reached the town's first main crossroads. In groups of six and eight men two battalions branched off along side-streets, keeping close to the walls of houses, while the other two battalions continued along the main road to the centre of the town.

Then, suddenly, the firing started in earnest. It seemed that hours must have passed since Falco's explosion, but Wilde's watch told him only three minutes had elapsed. He wondered what had taken the *fascisti* so long. The shots were coming in heavy, but spasmodic, bursts from houses along both sides of the street. On shouted commands from Wilde, groups of partisans fell out to contain the enemy fire, while the main body, in two files, continued towards the town centre. As they approached the main square the enemy fire thickened, and came solidly from the entire mass of buildings ahead of them.

Wilde noticed that the fire of his own men was often as ill-directed as the enemy's, but he argued that this was no time to risk cooling the partisans' ardour with reprimands for their sloppy aim.

News reached Wilde that the small groups of men along the side-streets were also encountering pockets of strong resistance, which slowed their progress—but the real battle would certainly develop in the town centre. The enemy machine-guns seemed to have taken a little time to come into action, and it occurred to Wilde that the officer in charge of the garrison could not have realized at first just what sort of an attack was taking place. But once the machine-guns did open up their fire, in well-directed arcs, they kept the partisans pinned down, and it was a dangerous game for a partisan to scuttle across to the other side of the street.

The advance was now considerably slowed, and Wilde could see how some men more than others were suited to this house-to-house street fighting. The trained soldiers were quick to show their expertise—making the most of any tiny amount of cover, flattening themselves against the wall to reduce the targets they offered, sprinting on split-second reflexes from doorway to doorway as a burst of machine-gun fire ceased and before the trigger could again be squeezed. Among the non-soldiers he noticed how much more ably the townsmen adapted themselves to these conditions, while the poachers, hunters, and mountaineers, who had excelled on previous occasions, were now plainly outclassed.

"And so the battle progressed," says Wilde. "All movement was dangerous and difficult. The strain was enormous. The slightest sign of life—and machine-gun bullets sprayed into the road and walls of the houses. Naturally we fired back, as we dodged forward, a doorway at a time—but it was painfully slow and exhausting. The sun rose higher in the sky, and the sweat poured from our bodies."

Mopping up in the side-streets was relatively simple, and soon all the partisans were concentrated on the town centre. Resistance there was based on three buildings: the Municipio (the town hall), the principal school, and the Castello—Varzi's official prison. Wilde did not know the identity of the enemy commander, except that it was neither Fiorentini nor Pastorelli, but possession of these three buildings afforded his opponent a certain freedom of movement in the eastern end of the town. Wilde called a council of war with Rossa and the other two battalion commanders. They agreed that the attack would have to be intensified. This would mean casualties, they knew, but the three enemy strongholds had to be taken, one by one. First, however, Wilde passed on the order that the men should have a brief rest and get whatever refreshment they could from the houses where they were sheltering.

It was about noon when the next phase of the attack began, with Primola Rossa leading half a dozen marksmen to a position from which they could cover any enemy movement between the Municipio and the school. As they dashed along a stretch of open pavement one man fell dead and another was shot through the arm, but the remaining five were unhurt. A few minutes later Wilde took a group of similar size out of cover, then back again—to give the enemy the impression they were trying to establish a new position to the left of the square. His real purpose, however, was to attract attention away from a much larger detachment that was filtering to the right of the square in order to start mopping-up operations at the far end of the town.

So the day continued. It was hot and heavy, but the courage and determination of the partisans remained high, and Wilde was reassured to see that his men's aim with *mitra*, rifle, and hand-grenade improved progressively as the day wore on. There were casualties on both sides, the partisan dead and wounded falling for the most part in the streets, while the *fascisti* were usually hit as they strayed across a window or doorway, or when a handful of partisans stormed a house from which they were firing.

An important figure in the battle was Don Tino. He did

not wait for lulls in the firing, but ran, pale-faced but serene, from street to street to tend the wounded and negotiate individual surrenders.

The dominant building in the square was the large, dark grey Municipio, its three storeys of tall windows topped by a curiously angled roof that gave a pagoda effect. It had the traditional wide balcony for the reading of the Duce's announcements, barred windows on the ground floor showing where prisoners awaiting trial were kept, and the customary flight of steps leading to a doorless archway. The school was almost entirely protected by the Municipio, and the fire from the latter was sufficiently intense to make a frontal assault impossible. There remained the Castello. Wilde reckoned that, for all its fortifications, it should prove an easier target, by virtue of its being hemmed in tightly by close-packed houses set in winding streets. And so it proved.

During the early afternoon news reached Wilde that the partisans were now almost completely in command of the eastern end of the town. The enemy were isolated in their three buildings in the main square.

Says Wilde: "I summoned Rossa and twenty men. The streets leading to the Castello offered such good cover before opening on to the square that I decided to lead a frontal assault. When you make an on-the-spot decision like that you don't stop to consider the consequences. You take a deep breath and jump in the deep end.

"That's what we did. Six men fell—four killed outright; one other was to die of his wounds—but the rest of us made it. And then, in a minute—no more—it was over. The troops inside the Castello surrendered.

"I nominated a small number of men to garrison the Castello, feeling strangely excited and exhilarated, as though I was drunk. I remember regretting that we didn't have bayonets. That, I felt, would have been a real charge.

"A couple of seconds later I became aware of how tired I was—and appreciated that the men must be feeling weary too. I told Rossa that I would postpone the rest of the attack until morning.

"A partisan came up to me and said that although the lines had been cut the telephone exchange could still be used to connect certain buildings inside the town. I made sure the school and Municipio were not directly connected with one another, then allowed my men to have a bit of fun by putting through ribald and mocking calls to the two buildings. Finally I took the phone myself and spoke to the major in charge of the town, whose headquarters were in the school. It was a strange sensation talking to the man I would have been quite happy to kill. I asked him to surrender. Very politely he refused.

"I was disappointed that success had not been more rapid, particularly since it would only be a matter of time before Voghera investigated the failure of the Varzi telephone lines, discovered the truth, and sent a relief force. It was with this danger in mind that I enforced the night's blockade of the two enemy buildings with just one of my five battalions, sending three others to the outskirts of the town to reinforce the defensive rôle that Falco's battalion had been impatiently filling.

"During the night there was desultory firing, but it seemed that the enemy was also anxious to get some rest. My last thoughts before falling asleep were for the civilian population of Varzi. I wondered how they were reacting to our assault—and it came to me that I'd not seen one civilian on the streets that day. Wisely they'd stayed well indoors."

Chapter
ELEVEN

The Battle of Varzi: Second Day

EARLY in the morning of October 16th Wilde ordered his men to return to the centre of the town. They took up positions behind cover and opened fire on the Municipio, but the return fire was equally heavy. A few impatient and impetuous partisans tried to get close enough to hurl grenades, but the accuracy of the enemy machine-guns soon sent them rushing back to shelter. Wilde noticed that the enemy fire was more disciplined than it had been the previous day, and in addition the force in the school started to open fire with a small mortar. This made his chances of gaining a quick infantry victory even remoter than they had been the previous day.

His own mortar was a much heavier weapon than the one in the school. Falco had established himself in the hills that overlooked the north of the town. He was little over half a mile from the Municipio—well within range. "But I was worried about the accuracy of both the mortar and its crew," says Wilde. "I didn't want mortar shells causing casualties among the civilian population. So I sent a messenger to Falco and had him bring the mortar right in close: on the roof of the Castello. I felt that at a range of only a hundred yards the risk to outsiders was minimal. My signal was a raised handkerchief: when I lowered my arm Falco opened fire."

The shell seemed to curve slowly into the air before dropping plumb centre into the Municipio roof.

The effect was remarkable. The entire Fascist force came rushing from the building, hands high in the air. To Wilde's surprise, there were only forty of them, and he felt he had to congratulate them on their dogged and spirited defence. For their part they were amazed that their reception was so pleasant—they had been fed for a long time on horror stories of what would happen to them if they fell into partisan hands. They admitted that it was fear of torture that had inspired them to fight so desperately. Without wasting further time Wilde had them sent under escort to Castagnola, and turned the mortar's attention to the school.

This time its first shot fell wide, landing nearer to the Municipio. The second was better placed, dropping just outside the school's main door. But its explosion was cushioned by a patch of grass and gravel and did little damage. Wilde signalled to Falco to cease firing—the near miss had given him an idea.

He called Don Rino and asked the priest if he would be prepared to take a message to the school, saying he would be the best emissary since he had the protection of his cloth. The *fascisti* could surely be relied upon not to shoot down an unarmed priest. Don Rino brushed these reassurances aside. He would go: that was that.

Wilde told Don Rino that he wanted him to contact the major in command of the enemy force and explain to him how hopeless his position was, emphasizing the stranglehold the partisans held on the town. He should then invite him to meet Wilde half-way between the school and the Municipio, unarmed, and in full view of both sides.

The partisans ceased firing, a white flag was waved—and the priest squared his shoulders and walked out. Mercifully the *fascisti* held their fire. Wilde saw him approach the school, watched as the door opened and the priest went inside. . . . A few minutes later he reappeared, and brought Wilde the news that the major had agreed to a parley.

"I unbuckled my revolver belt," he says, "while some of the men around me expressed grave doubts as to the wisdom of my action. They were certain that the *fascisti*, ever treacherous, had some dirty trick up their sleeves. To some extent I shared their anxiety, but I'd committed myself and could hardly turn back. But I did agree to the suggestion that Don Rino should accompany me as an extra guarantee.

"By now it was getting towards the end of the afternoon, and what had been a warm day was turning into a bright, cold evening, with the first hint of approaching winter.... The town seemed to be utterly silent. I recall noticing that even the birds seemed to have abandoned us—and one of the features of the fighting had been their agitated chirruping and flying from tree to tree. I think most of this silence was in my mind rather than anywhere else, but at the time it was ominous and sinister. My tenseness communicated itself to my men as I walked slowly with Don Rino to the gates of the school.

"The major was standing there, awaiting us. I came to a halt about twenty yards away and called for the Fascist commander to come over to us."

Wilde found himself facing a short, slim Italian of about thirty, with a three-day growth of beard and an untidy and incomplete uniform. His general air of scruffiness seemed to reflect a pessimistic awareness of defeat. He greeted the two partisans with a polite "Good evening" and offered his hand. Neither accepted it.

"I am in charge of partisan operations in this town," said Wilde, clasping his hands behind his back, quarter-deck fashion. "How long do you think you can hold out?"

"Long enough." The major smiled. "One of my men escaped through your blockade during the night—about twelve hours ago. He will have reached Voghera by now. Help is on the way. I fear that Varzi will soon be your trap and not your prize."

Swiftly, Wilde's mind considered the major's words. The soldier might well be lying, attempting a desperate—if courageous—bluff. On the other hand it could well be true, in which case the partisans would be in a desperate position. But in the final analysis the danger of a relief force from Voghera existed, whether the major was bluffing or not—had existed ever since the telephone lines were cut.

Wilde smiled, and shook his head. "That must have been the man we caught. He wouldn't tell us where he was going, so we shot him."

The major raised his eyebrows, but said nothing.

"I have more than five hundred men besieging this town," Wilde continued—knowing that the major could have no idea of the true number of men that had been based on Castagnola. "There is no chance of any relief force coming through. Our ambushes will decimate them on the road. Indeed, why did we attack Varzi in the first place? Think about it and you'll realize that our assault was designed to lure the Germans back. Varzi is no more than a bait. So your position is hopeless. Either way, whether you surrender now or are killed, you cannot hope to win—or expect to be saved by your German friends. I am prepared to offer you and your men safe passage out of Varzi, rather than imprisonment, as a gesture of appreciation for your gallant defence. But you must surrender all your arms and equipment—and I want a quick answer."

The major nodded. "May I have permission to return to my men? I will ask them what they wish to do—although for my part I shall stay put and fight it out, single-handed if necessary."

Both sides withdrew, and met again after an interval of five minutes—five long minutes in which Wilde prayed hard that the enemy would accept his terms of surrender. But Wilde could tell from the major's bearing—erect now and proud—that it was not to be. "I have the honour to inform you," he said, "that my men have decided to carry on the fight. I remain in full legal command of Varzi." He turned on his heel, but before he could walk off he was stopped by Wilde's voice.

"All right, so you stay—and die. In any case you are short of water, since the mains to the school have been shut. I am sending my men to the *alberghi* to eat, and to drink all the wine they want. Think of this—and don't forget to tell your troops."

Wilde and Don Rino returned towards the Municipio.

Wilde was acutely aware of the defencelessness of his back and felt his shoulder blades contract. He struggled hard not to increase his pace. Although the *fascisti* did not break the truce, they were quick on the trigger as soon as Wilde and the priest reached the corner of the Municipio: a mortar shell burst almost at their feet as they joined up again with Primola Rossa. Fortunately, none of them was hurt.

Wilde signalled to Falco to reopen his attack on the school. The first shot fell wide. The second was better aimed, and dropped close to the previous near miss. The next was right on target and blew a gaping, rubble-spewing hole in the roof of the school. Now that the range had been established, every shot went home. One struck the front wall of the school a glancing blow, twisting out a large metal window-frame and uprooting a tree—causing it to fall heavily against the shattered window. Another must have penetrated three floors before exploding, for it blew out an entire wall of basement windows.

Six hits plunged in rapid succession into the building, and Wilde wondered for how much longer the garrison could hold out. Each mortar shot was punctuated by a burst of firing from the school, but its volume decreased with every hit. Says Wilde: "I toyed with the idea of calling off the attack until morning, letting hunger and thirst work out the solution for me, or forcing a conclusion that evening by leading a charge. I was about to settle for the latter when my attention was drawn back to the school by the shouts of the men near me. A white tablecloth was fluttering from an upstair window. The garrison had surrendered, and the battle of Varzi was over."

Wilde signalled to Falco to cease firing. He was glad it was over, not only because he had gained a splendid victory, but also because the cold-blooded reduction of the school to dust and ashes was not the sort of fighting that appealed to him.

He marshalled the men around him and made them line the square. He went to meet the *fascisti*, who were led by the major, despite his earlier vow to fight on alone. Arms and ammunition were piled in the school's playground, and the garrison looked for the most part as sad as demoralized. He ordered them to line up, but told the major he could stay by his side. The major refused and joined his men. There were a hundred and ten of them. This meant that the partisans had faced a total force—including the forty prisoners taken from the Municipio and the sixty they had captured in the streets or killed—of about two hundred: a number less than their own, and therefore quite a new experience.

Wilde addressed the prisoners, and repeated his offer of a safe conduct through the town and its outer ring of partisan defences as far as the road to Voghera. He added that his Aliotta Division would welcome to its ranks any men who had fought against them purely out of loyalty to the army and not because they were Fascists. He emphasized that some of his best men had recently served in the army, but they realized they best helped their country by fighting against the *fascisti*, not with them. He asked if any man would like to fight against the German oppressors and the Fascists. Wilde knew that the invitation would appeal to those soldiers who wanted no more than a chance to desert and return to their homes, but this did not worry him—it still meant that many less fighting for the enemy.

There was a pause. The major looked at his men with some agitation. Then a grizzled sergeant-major stepped forward and said he had no wish to go to Voghera. The spell was broken. In a matter of seconds about half the men came forward and offered to join the partisans. Without further delay Wilde had an escort accompany the major and the rest of his detachment to the Voghera road, then detailed some men from Falco's battalion to accompany the new recruits back to Castagnola. He reasoned that the sooner they were back at base the better; he would have enough problems on his hands at Varzi without the worry of fifty new men of untested loyalty.

So the day was won, and the town was theirs. The coup that for so long had seemed a dream was now undeniable reality. Wilde was on the threshold of vast new problems as well as tremendous opportunities. And even though the winning of Varzi was certainly the greatest achievement recorded in that part of Italy, he did not feel excited.

"Partly," says Wilde, "it was sheer physical weariness. But more than that, the manner of victory was not that which I would have wished. For the first time in months I reacted against the noisy, exaggerated, and tasteless manner in which the Italians rejoiced and celebrated. I refused the bottle of wine that was thrust into my hand, and called my lieutenants for a council. I thanked them, told them to make certain discipline was maintained, and ordered that the outposts round the town must be fully and conscientiously manned. I told them that while they could celebrate if they wished, I was going to bed. Which I did—only to lie awake and regret bitterly my boorishness."

For their part, his lieutenants contented themselves with a smile and a shrug as they left the Municipio. Gems was tired, and no wonder. . . .

Celebrations engulfed the entire town, civilian and partisan alike. There was drinking and singing and love-making and innumerable speeches. The great cry of one innkeeper was: "*E cessato l'infausto regno del terrore, e tornata la liberta!*" ("The infamous reign of terror is ended, and liberty has returned!") —which came oddly from a man notorious for his sycophancy.

A few gave thanks to God, and the name of Don Tino was mentioned in many prayers. But it was the celebrative element which predominated, and it was dawn before the last groups of partisans and townsfolk staggered arm in arm from the taverns, shouting a last "*Vittoria!*" ("Victory!") into the cold air of the streets.

And in the Municipio the man who had led them to victory and freedom finally slept.

When he awoke Wilde went for a walk around the town. He was distressed and enraged by what he saw—there was evidence of looting. When he returned to the Municipio a delegation of the town's tradesmen awaited him. It transpired that the looting was still going on, and although the partisans said they were only making the Fascists and their sympathizers suffer, there was proof that much of the looting was quite indiscriminate.

Wilde's temper flared, and he demanded an immediate meeting of his lieutenants. They arrived sleepy-eyed and plainly suffering from hangovers, but he soon startled them into clear-headed consciousness. He gave them all a severe tongue-lashing, and asked what further reliance he could ever place on them if they were incapable of carrying out his simple instruction to see that discipline was maintained in the town. As he heard himself speak he discovered that, completely unintentionally and without effort, he sounded like an authoritarian commander berating his junior officers on a quarterdeck. He sensed, too, that, despite the free-and-easy nature of partisan service, there was as little likelihood of his juniors answering back in that office in the Municipio as in the Royal Navy.

Wilde went on to tell them that it would not be enough merely to issue further instructions and warnings. Firm steps would have to be taken. Firstly, two-thirds of the partisan force would leave Varzi and occupy positions in the hills between the town and Castagnola. Not only would this deal with the indiscipline; it would dispose a large part of the division in positions from which they could most effectively be deployed in the event of a counter-attack. Secondly, a force of 'policemen' would be appointed from among the more responsible partisans. They would come under his personal control, and would stop any partisan from entering private premises without authority. Thirdly, there would be a ten-thirty curfew, at which time all taverns would be closed. Only policemen, sentries, and official patrols would be allowed on the streets after 11 P.M.

To his surprise, this new discipline was not only accepted and adhered to, but won the approval of the majority of his men.

"But I continued to suffer from the depression I had felt on the night of the capture of Varzi," says Wilde, "and tried to probe my own mind to discover the cause. It was not that I was worried about the future of Varzi. Winter was coming—

traditionally a period of stalemate as far as partisan activities were concerned. Guerrilla warfare in the mountains depended on speed and manœuvrability—and both these elements were destroyed when the snows came. But, even apart from the weather, I knew we were not equipped to hold the town against a full-scale enemy attempt to regain it. I had known this from the start, and my plans for the future went no further than inflicting the maximum amount of casualties on the enemy before retiring to the hills and mountains until the spring.

"My depression stemmed from something else. Mainly, I think, because I could see no further heights to climb. For months the taking of Varzi had been my ultimate aim; my absolute, as it were. Now this had been achieved, what new target could be set—taking into consideration the approach of winter and the practical limitations of my relatively small force? There seemed to be none.

"And from this sense of anticlimax came an overwhelming nostalgia—not for England, or Sheffield, or the Navy, but for the via Sant' Ambrogio in Voghera and for Teresa and Giuseppe. I don't know why this should have been the case, but it was."

Restless, bored, Wilde had to find some focal point of concentration, and for some odd reason discovered it in a consuming desire to learn what had happened to his friends in Voghera. And so he summoned Primola Rossa and told him to take temporary command of the town while he went off on a reconnaissance "which might last several days".

He set off on foot. He walked partly along the main road and partly in the relative shelter of the fields or river-beds. His mood was such that he was not perhaps as alert as he ought to have been; his one compulsive thought was to get to Voghera. He had little fear of being recognized and apprehended in the town after so many months. Although he was armed, he did not look like the popular conception of a victorious partisan commander—and in any case would hide his weapons before reaching Voghera, where he would simply melt into the crowd. He felt confident that he would encounter no difficulties. Indeed, nearer to the town he would hitch a lift in a lorry or car.

He walked for two hours until he was past Bagnaria and approaching Ponte Nizza. For no positive reason he decided to make a detour to the north of the main road and cut across the minor road that ran from Ponte Nizza to Zavattarello. Crossing the fields at the back of the houses, he followed a narrow cart-track that led past a derelict old barn before turning west again and heading for the minor road.

He had just reached the corner of the barn when its door opened. He caught sight of a group of men—a Fascist patrol.

Instinctively, forgetting his newly assumed rôle of the harmless, innocent civilian, Wilde pulled his revolver from the waistband of his trousers.

Before he could fire the door of the barn was slammed shut and rifle-shots came from its upper windows. He backed away, hesitated for a split-second, then turned and ran.

"Suddenly," says Wilde, "my right arm spun upwards as though of its own volition. I had time to wonder why it should do this, then realized I had been hit. An intense, burning pain pierced my right shoulder.

"My first feeling was that I was going to die . . . that I was dead. . . . But I kept on running. . . . I dropped my revolver, turned to grab it with my left hand, then dashed on towards a small gully. Its incline must have been steeper than I realized, for before I knew what was happening I tumbled head over heels into it. My shoulder hurt like hell, and I had no time to collect my wits and think intelligently. I didn't know what to do first: nurse my shoulder, get my breath back, try to think—or pray. In a moment of near panic I almost burst into tears at what I considered to be the unfairness of it all."

A few seconds later his priorities were decided for him. He heard a rush of feet and the chatter of excited voices. The patrol was scrambling at the top of the gully. Death was only a moment away as Wilde remembered the single German grenade in his jacket pocket. Sobbing now, he jerked it free with his left hand and pushed the string loop with its small button attachment into his mouth. At the top of the gully he saw the six or eight—God knows how many of them—peering down. His teeth snapped tight on the thin cord, and he pulled hard with his left hand. Without even attempting to aim he hurled the grenade towards what appeared to be a vast mass of faces and uniforms.

He was briefly aware of them trying to scatter before the grenade landed among them, but without stopping to see the devastation it caused he was out of the far end of the gully, running as fast as his legs would carry him. He remembers covering a few paces before hearing noise, all sorts of noise, including the screams of the patrol and the explosion of the grenade—and the bark of his revolver, which, automatically, he was firing behind him as he went.

He ran . . . and ran . . . and ran, until his heart thumped in an agonizing tattoo against his chest and his breath came in hoarse, painful, choking gasps. And still he ran.

After a while he became aware of footsteps behind him. But they were some distance away—and seemed to grow fainter as he rushed blindly on. He could not afford to stop and listen, but headed roughly eastward, keeping parallel to the main road on its northern side. He staggered past rocky outcrops, struggled through thorn hedges, and banged past the sides of trees. His body was torn and scratched and bruised, and his shoulder was still throbbing and burning—but worse than all these was the agony of his strained lungs. Finally, in a small but dense group of trees, he slumped headlong to the ground . . . and stayed there.

Slowly the thumping of his heart eased, and his breath came more normally. He was able to listen—but could hear no sound of pursuit. He half walked, half crawled to a vantage-point at the top of the copse—but there was no sign of movement.

He worked out his position and started back towards Varzi, every step sending a spasm of pain through the upper half of his body.

Chapter
TWELVE

The Family Camporotunda

FOUR hours later Wilde reached the first partisan outpost and was carried to the town's hospital, a small building run by six nuns and the eighty-year-old Dr Benzoni. And so began yet another phase of the Englishman's life.

For the first few days after the operation for the removal of the bullet he felt weak from loss of blood. Then, as his strength returned, he began to enjoy the enforced laziness. The long wire cage over his arm and the weighted pulley leading over the front of the bed restricted his movements, but the nuns made him their immediate favourite—and in view of his position among the partisans there was no suggestion of enforcing proper visiting hours. Indeed, the flow of well-wishers became so great that Wilde had to tell Primola Rossa and the sister in charge of the ward to restrict their number. One thing he found particularly delightful was the way that the outlying villages would choose a singularly beautiful young *signorina* to bring their offerings of cakes, sweets, or fruit.

During his second week in hospital Dr Benzoni said that he was a little worried as to whether Wilde's arm would set properly. By means which he refused to disclose (and which Primola Rossa assured him had nothing to do with the partisans) the old doctor succeeded in bringing a professor of orthopædics from as far away as Alessandria. The professor had with him a different type of wire cage, which had to be placed under Wilde's arm in such a way that the arm was kept at a right angle to the body. This introduced new discomfort, and made proper sleep impossible for the first few days; but Wilde was soon well enough to start taking short walks in the hospital grounds.

His encounter with the patrol had achieved one useful purpose: it had erased his mood of depression—although he was still disenchanted with the business of being a partisan commander. Primola Rossa was his most frequent visitor, and kept him posted with news. There was still no sign of enemy counter-attacks against Varzi, and, unlike Wilde, Rossa did not feel the need for new peaks to climb. He was happy to organize and participate in routine daily patrols, accepting the fact that the partisans would have to travel a long way from Varzi if they were to find action against the enemy.

Wilde learned that there were many new faces among the partisan force in the town. Their victory had attracted groups of men from Zavattarello, Capanette di Pej, and areas even farther afield. Wilde was not certain whether they wanted recruits who flitted irresponsibly from one division to another, some because they wanted to share the glory of having served with the Aliotta partisans—others, he felt sure, Communists sent to try to infiltrate into the administration of the first town of any size seized from the enemy. But he argued that this was no time to question loyalties or cause disharmony in the ranks.

One day he had something approaching the shock of his life: sitting in bed, he heard English voices, and two British army sergeants were brought in to see him. For a moment Wilde thought the Allied armies had arrived, then dismissed the thought as quickly as it came—his patrols would certainly have been aware of any such advance. It transpired that the two men had escaped from a prisoner-of-war camp to the north, and were attempting to make their way back to the Allied lines.

"We chatted for two hours," says Wilde, "and the sound of English voices brought back a flood of longings and memories that I had carefully kept locked away. I was very close to tears. I wished I was fit enough to accompany them, but knew that in my present state I would have been a burden rather than a help. I had to content myself with making sure they were provided with food and maps and escorted on their way by one of my patrols.

"One odd thing about the meeting was the way in which I had to get used to speaking English again. I had spoken Italian, and thought in Italian, for so long, my English came hesitatingly, and almost sounded like a foreign language!"

Soon after this visit three Americans came to see him. They belonged to a special service unit engaged on sabotage behind the enemy lines. Nine of them had been dropped in the mountains above Pej, although more to hinder the German retreat than to aid partisan activity. At the moment they were exploring the area before getting down to real work. Their leader, known simply as "Captain Bill", loaded Wilde with chewing-gum and candy from his rucksack, and asked him if he was prepared, when fit again, to act as their interpreter and guide. Wilde declined, and the Americans expressed amazement that he should choose to stay among foreigners. With a smile Wilde assured them that he was able to look after himself, and added that it would have been a help if one of their number had been able to speak Italian and so dispense with the need for an interpreter.

Another visitor was Domenico, the cousin of Serafina whom Wilde had first met at Pozzol Groppo. Wilde was pleased to see him again, and moved to think that news of his mishap had brought him all the way across country to Varzi. But Domenico said that his real purpose in coming was to persuade Wilde to give up his life as a partisan for the duration of the winter and come and live with the family at Pozzol Groppo. There he would be both safe and reasonably comfortable. Says Wilde: "The offer was certainly sincere, but it meant returning to that old semi-captivity. I was determined to retain my freedom of movement. . . .

"One question I continually asked myself was whether I might have lost my nerve. Whether or not I led my partisans into battle again, was I really capable of doing so? Was that the real reason for my depression and restlessness? Only time could answer these questions. My immediate aim was to get out and about—I was really terrified at the thought of the enemy seizing the town with me lying helpless in a hospital bed."

Within the next few days Wilde was allowed outside the hospital gates. In the streets he was greeted with cheers and hand-clasps wherever he went, truly a return of the conquering hero. One of his first calls, after he had made certain the military and civilian administration of Varzi was as it should be, was to the Camporotunda family.

Carlo Camporotunda, the eldest son and now head of the family, had been one of his partisans ever since Wilde had taken over at Castagnola. His two brothers, Bruno and Ottavio, were still at school, but had come into their own with the capture of Varzi, acting as Primola Rossa's personal messengers. Their father had been shot by the Fascists for no specific reason at the time of the battle of Dego. His widow, a tall angular woman, carried her sorrow with quiet dignity, and continued to run the little general shop in the main square. And there were four daughters: Rosina, Giovannina, Maria, and Nina, ranging in age from twenty-five to eleven. Giovannina was already known to him, since she had been a frequent visitor at the hospital, where she insisted on polishing his boots and taking away his clothes for cleaning and repair, and sitting at his feet while he told her his life-story.

For their own part the girls also had many stories to tell. The family had been actively anti-Fascist since the signing of the Armistice. On one occasion Fiorentini suspected—rightly—that they had aided an escaped British officer as he slipped through the enemy defences. Lacking proof, and failing in his attempts to bully an admission from the family, he sent the girls to the Voghera lunatic asylum, presumably in the hope that they would soon confess rather than remain in such an establishment. But the girls held out, and after a month Fiorentini signed the order for their release. They were able to laugh at their experiences, and it was Giovannina's party piece to give imitations of the behaviour of some of the asylum's inmates.

It became clear to Wilde that Giovannina had taken a strong liking to him. He told her he was engaged to be married, but the tall, dark-haired girl seemed not to understand.

Soon Wilde's shoulder started itching, which led him to think the wound must be healing. He got the nuns to strip off his bandages, only to discover that the irritation was caused by lice.

But the shoulder did start to heal—just as news reached Wilde that there were signs of enemy activity around Varzi. Dr Benzoni told him there was no reason why he should not return to active service—although he would still need to wear the cage on his arm—so long as he reported to the hospital for regular checks.

It was rumoured that parachutists were to land near Varzi. The reason for this, Wilde was told, was not a direct counter-attack to recapture the town, but stemmed from a daring coup carried out by Americano and a detachment of his Third Lombardia Division. It appeared that a certain Colonel Tropp, the Germans' senior mechanical engineering specialist in Italy, and the key man in many of the enemy's plans, was to pass through Voghera. It was a tribute to Americano's daring and to his intelligence service, that he not only knew precise details of Tropp's movements, but was able to intercept the colonel and whisk him away to the mountains to the north-east of Zavattarello. What happened to him there—whether he was held prisoner or killed—no one seemed to know. But it was said that parachutists were to drop to the north of Varzi as part of the search for the missing man. During the next few days aircraft did, in fact, fly low over the valleys, but Wilde's patrols found no positive proof that men had been dropped.

After this scare had died down Wilde had a visitor at the Municipio, a partisan leader from the mountains beyond the Penice Pass near Bobbio. His name was Eduardo, and he had come to ask Wilde for his help. A small British parachute unit, men from the Special Air Service, were engaged in building up a cache of weapons and equipment near where Eduardo's division was operating. Its purpose was similar to that of Captain Bill—to prepare to attack the Germans when the retreat reached that part of the country. This meant, in turn, that they were in no way concerned with partisan activities, no matter how praiseworthy, except to express a passing, almost academic, interest. Eduardo's plea was that Wilde should return with him and attempt to persuade the British soldiers to part with a token amount of arms and ammunition. The British officer, he explained, spoke virtually no Italian, and, despite his own knowledge of English, Eduardo was getting nowhere with the SAS unit.

Wilde knew it would be a wasted journey, for even if the SAS could be made to see the vital work against the enemy that was being performed by the partisans, they had to obey orders: arms built up for one specific purpose could hardly be found to be missing when the time came for their stated use. Yet Eduardo was a likeable man, and, rather than appear to be unco-operative, Wilde agreed to accompany him.

"It would have been a strenuous journey at the best of times," says Wilde. "A ridge of almost four thousand feet had to be crossed. Now, with the approach of winter, it was bitterly cold, and the streams we had to ford were strong-running and icy. I forced myself to keep to Eduardo's pace despite the cage on my arm.

"The British officer was amiable enough—but adamant. The best I could do was get a promise that if I gave him details of partisan activities in the area he would radio them back to British headquarters in the hope that supplies of arms would be flown out to us. I did this, but had no great expectations of the outcome.

"Inevitably I had to explain how it was that I, an Englishman, came to be commanding a brigade of partisans deep in the mountains. But I did not prolong the discussion: I had no desire to revive the longings and nostalgia that came with speaking English.

"I returned to Varzi without too much difficulty, and

found that the exercise had done my arm not harm, but good. Dr Benzoni told me I could exchange the cage for a sling."

A few days later, while Primola Rossa was away from Varzi on patrol, Wilde heard rifle and machine-gun fire from the north. Minutes later a messenger came running up. His news was grave: somehow a strong German armoured column had penetrated to the north and east of Varzi without being spotted by the Aliotta sentries or patrols. It seemed as though it had been scouring the withdrawal area of the Third Lombardia Division behind Zavattarello, possibly in search of the missing colonel. In any event it was now heading down the road from Zavattarello to Varzi, and the firing that could be heard was an exchange between the enemy and the partisan outpost that had finally sighted them.

Wilde's force in Varzi numbered less than a hundred men, and there was no time to prepare the sort of ambush that allowed a force of this size to take on a massively superior enemy. Wilde cursed the inefficiency of his patrols, and decided that the rapid evacuation of the town was more than a matter of prudence—it was the only course of action left to him. Again the mobility and speed of the partisans proved their salvation—within minutes the town was left to the apprehensive civilians.

Wilde had instructed his men to re-form at Castagnola, and was furious at the general lack of order and discipline he found among the holding force there. He rapidly set to work to put matters right. The following morning he learned that the German column had stayed only overnight at Varzi before taking the road back to Voghera. "There was no reason why we should not reoccupy Varzi," he says, "and we did so, having been away for just over twenty-four hours. The rushing away, then hurrying back, has a farcical element in retrospect, but it was a grim and desperate manœuvre at the time."

For another fortnight events continued to observe the usual pattern, with the significant difference that clashes between the patrols and the enemy became increasingly frequent. It meant straining resources to the utmost to ensure there were sufficient patrols in the field to do battle with the enemy. As before, the partisans almost invariably got the better of these clashes, and it was also significant that the enemy was made up of a larger proportion of Germans than hitherto. Wilde devoted as much time as he could to helping establish a civil régime in Varzi made up of non-Fascists—no easy task with the town full of jealousies, accusations, recriminations, and dubious loyalties. His arm became progressively less stiff, and towards the end of November a series of X-rays satisfied Dr Benzoni that it was sufficiently healed for Wilde to dispense with the bandages and sling.

It became clear that the Voghera command was now conducting a systematic combing of the hills, and the partisans were aware that for the first time in many months the battle was being carried to them. Then intelligence reached Wilde from Voghera that these local sweeps were part of something bigger. German units were operating out of Stradella, Tortona, Alessandria, and Novi Ligure, as well as Voghera—the beginning of the big winter push they had all been expecting. It was coming—deliberately—at a time when the partisans were at their weakest for fighting back. Forced to retreat into the mountain snows, they would not be able to venture forth again until the following spring. Properly handled, the offensive would guarantee the German rear for the whole of the winter. Psychologically, too, the partisans were unprepared to resist the push, and Wilde was informed that all the divisions in the area were falling back on Capannette di Pej.

"Again I wondered at the tremendous, almost magical, reputation this village had in the thinking of the partisans, and I hoped it would be big enough to accommodate all the people going there. Without delay and without argument—for if the entire division from Primola Rossa downwards wanted to go I could hardly stop them—we abandoned Varzi and marched to Pej. It was now the beginning of December 1944, and the Aliotta force was down to about two hundred and fifty men. . . . And three women."

The three were the eldest Camporotunda girls, Rosina,

Giovannina, and sixteen-year-old Maria. For the previous few weeks they had been acting as the partisans' cooks, and their hatred of everything German and Fascist was so great that they insisted on continuing to assist their "brave brothers in the field". Wilde wondered whether they would slow down the overall speed of the march, but he discovered that their standards of fitness and mountaincraft were higher than those of many of the male partisans.

At Pej Wilde found that Captain Bill had gone, and the remaining Americans were prepared to hand over two or three thousand hand-grenades and several hundred pounds' weight of high explosive, a gift of enormous value in terms of future operations. As soon as they arrived the partisans set to work building a series of fortifications. These would serve two purposes: to provide defensive cover for the ambushing of an enemy force proceeding up the valley and to safeguard the now considerable store of arms and ammunition hidden in the *capannette*. The material they used was local stone, and the work was hard and tiring. Nor were their spirits improved by learning that enemy forces occupied Varzi the day after they left. It suggested the Germans were well acquainted with partisan movements—although Wilde wondered why they had not attacked the town while his troops were there. One answer was extremely flattering to the partisans' reputation as fighters.

There was only a handful of other partisans at Pej when they arrived, and even with these, balancing those of Wilde's force who had decided they would be better off spending the winter at home on their farms, it still meant the Aliotta Division totalled no more than two hundred and fifty men. And despite the reports that all the partisan groups in the area were converging on Pej, none came.

The next shock came when Wilde's patrols discovered that the nearest enemy forces were not in the process of marching up the valley towards the partisan ambush positions—they were already poised in the mountains *above* Pej. The threat would come from the heights—and from specialist mountain troops at that.

Then a scout brought the information that a detachment of these troops, size unknown, was occupying a derelict watch-tower above Capannette di Pej in the Costa Montanaia ridge. Wilde decided to lead ten men, including Rossa, with a view to a possible attack. They reached the bastion at dusk, and waited in the chill air until it was completely dark. Wilde's plan was for seven members of the patrol to open fire from one side of the tower. After about a quarter of an hour they would retreat for a short distance, but give the impression that they had retired completely. Meanwhile Wilde, Rossa, and one other would have reached the blind side of the tower. . . . After that everything depended on whatever opportunities fortune offered.

The plan went smoothly, and luck was with them. For a minute or two the three men waited shivering against the smooth, unscalable wall of the tower, pressing themselves as close to it as they could, for they were a perfect target for a machine-gun. Edging their way along, they discovered a short flight of steps going down to a small door. By good fortune it was unlocked.

Moving quickly and silently, they entered the tower. The room in which they found themselves was clearly a disused cellar. They crouched there, waiting until the firing ended—then waited for a further five minutes to give the defenders time to relax and settle down. As long as their own patrol remained quiet, Wilde was confident that things would work out well. And they did.

At the end of the cellar was a staircase. Wilde mounted it, paused at the door at the top, and listened. He could hear voices and movement. In a frenzy of movement he opened the door and threw in three grenades. Then he pulled the door shut and backed away. The explosion in the confined space of the room was deafening, and seemed to make the entire tower totter for a moment. As soon as the noise died away the three men rushed in, *mitras* at the ready.

It transpired that there had been twelve men in the room. All had been killed, many blown into unrecognizable fragments. The six men in the room above surrendered without a fight—hurrying down with their hands high above their heads.

A small, but classic victory for the partisans.

Before withdrawing Wilde had the prisoners tied up and left in an open position where they would easily be spotted by their comrades. From his interrogation of them it became clear that heavy enemy pressure was going to be brought to bear on both Pej and Capannette di Pej. Primola Rossa insisted that their position was untenable. The only thing to do, he said, was withdraw to another part of the mountains.

Back at Capanette it was clear that the overwhelming majority of the partisan force sided with Rossa, and Wilde was compelled to fall in with the plan.

"It was the beginning of a nightmare," says Wilde. "Snow began to fall—a heavy, icy blanket that seemed to chill my soul as well as my bones. I really understood now why winter was the closed season in terms of partisan activity. We were a large body to be operating as one unit on difficult mountain terrain, and although Primola Rossa and several others knew the point for which we were heading, the snow was now swirling so strongly in the wind that it was impossible to distinguish landmarks, and even difficult to see the man in front. I felt thoroughly depressed and sick of the whole escapade. I was suffering bitterly from the cold. My arm started to pain me again, and I found myself wishing to high heaven that I was safe and warm in some prisoner-of-war camp.

"We rested for the night, covering ourselves with the thick blankets we had with us—but they were totally inadequate protection. We marched for the whole of the next day and well into the night. For food we forced lumps of iron-hard bread between our chattering teeth. We were still looking for somewhere to camp for the night when, to my horror, the weather became even worse.

"The wind rose, and it seemed that, despite all the storms I had encountered at sea, I'd never really known the true meaning of bad weather. For hours we battled on, each step a punishment. My feet would sink deep into the snow—as though sucked in and held tight—and had to be dragged free . . . step after step . . . hour after hour . . . and all the time the wind was like a million needles tearing at my face, and the cold ate deep down inside me."

It was almost midnight before the partisans reached the relative shelter of a group of blizzard-swept barns overhanging a small village two hundred feet below. They had stretched endurance to the limit—the half-dozen houses might offer food and warmth, but all they wanted now was rest. For some time the column had ceased to be an entity, a coherent whole, but was rather a straggling line of desperate, solitary units. They continued to stagger in throughout the night, and when morning came it was found that twenty men were still missing. There was little doubt of their fate: blown over unprotected rockfaces where the combination of wind, treacherous footholds, and physical fatigue had proved too great for them.

Despite the fact that they were wearing short skirts and had bare legs, the three Camporotunda sisters were in good spirits. Their cheerfulness, Wilde was certain, played a great part in keeping the general level of morale high—no man was anxious to reveal himself as less strong or spirited than three girls. To their credit, none of the girls would accept any form of special treatment; they marched and climbed through the blizzard, refusing all offers of help.

Apart from the girls, Wilde was greatly impressed by the leader of the small band of partisans he had found awaiting the Aliotta Division at Pej. It was he, next morning, who urged the column to an early start, bullying the late arrivals who had been able to snatch less than two hours' rest. He argued against a mass descent on the village—and his prudence was justified when a lone scout went out and returned with the information that more than two hundred heavily armed German mountain troops were billeted there. The heat was on with a vengeance. The partisans were in no condition to consider any kind of action against the enemy, and could only hurry away as fast as they were able—still weary and aching, their wet and icy clothes sticking to their bodies.

The snow was some three feet deep now, making progress even slower and more painful. The morning was not long advanced when it was discovered that somewhere along the line they had lost the solitary mule they had brought from Varzi. Since the animal was carrying their supply of food it was necessary to send a search-party back to find it. Luckily it was not far away, and miraculously, in the process of looking for it, they stumbled across the body of one of their lost comrades.

He must have blundered on past the barns, and was now a ghastly sight. His arms and legs were frozen quite solid, and he was in some sort of coma. They built a fire behind a bank of ice and tried to warm his limbs. They opened his clothes and rubbed his body with snow in an attempt to improve his circulation. But it was apparent to them all that there was little hope of him living.

They made a rough litter from the branches of trees and took turns carrying him. They battled on for the whole of that day, and again found shelter for the night in some barns. And so into the next day. "I don't know how we survived or found the strength to drag our bodies on," says Wilde. "God alone must know the answer. A step at a time . . . bent almost double . . . the pain, paradoxically, now so severe it could hardly be felt. Only one thing was agreed among us—that going farther into the mountains would prove merely suicidal. Our one hope lay in returning to the area around Varzi and dispersing to farms until the spring came."

On the fourth evening they reached the largest village they had come across since leaving Pej. A scout determined that it was free of German or Fascist troops, and the column dragged themselves into it, searching for warmth, food, and rest. Wilde took over the responsibility of finding a home for the man on the stretcher, and was disgusted with the reception he received. The village was outside the normal area of partisan activity, and its inhabitants felt none of the sympathy for the Garibaldini that existed in other parts of the region. On the contrary, they made it quite clear that they resented the coming of the partisans, asking why they should deliberately invite reprisals from the Germans or *fascisti*.

Wilde knocked at door after door, and was met with the same refusal of help. He was in despair when he found himself confronted by the village priest. "I have heard of your problem, my son," the white-haired old *parroco* said. "You should have come to me in the first place. Of course I will have him." Despite this kindness, and the efforts of the partisans, the man died the next day—after Wilde and his men had spent another night in the rough shelter of a group of barns.

"Even though the route we were now following took us east, then north, to a lower and less exposed terrain," continues Wilde, "there were still occasionally drifts up to eight feet deep to be struggled through. During the fifth day the wind rose again, and there were showers of driving hail. And all the time there was this murderous, biting cold. I cursed the weather and the War. I found myself wishing that we would meet some Germans and be forced to fight—to be killed or captured in an engagement that would at least warm the blood. We were exhausted . . . worn out . . . finished. My arm had become progressively worse, and I was virtually one-handed. I felt that I could not last for very much longer—and then I saw the Camporotunda sisters in a more grievous state than myself. Somehow, as the girls started lagging behind, I found some reserve of strength and went to their assistance, helping first one then another with my one good arm, and trying to make weak jokes to help build up their spirits."

That night the partisans halted as soon as it was dark, regardless of the fact that they were nowhere near a barn or a hut—or any other form of shelter. There just wasn't the strength of endurance to go any farther. By now they were scattered over a wide area, and individual groups set about making camp in the snow. The party Wilde was with totalled about twenty and included the Camporotunda sisters. They found a hollow and trod down the snow until it was hard and firm. Then they placed their blankets over it and huddled together as tightly as possible in an attempt to generate some communal warmth. Few of them were able to sleep even for a matter of minutes, and it was necessary for them to make sorties in groups of three or four to stamp their feet and swing their arms in order to keep the circulation going and create some feeling in their limbs. Next morning a further roll-call revealed that another fifteen men were missing from among the scattered groups. Although it was hoped that at least some of them had gone off in the night, making individual efforts to reach safety, not one of them was ever heard of again.

The retreat from Pej had proved to be a major catastrophe, and had inflicted more casualties on Wilde's division than had enemy action during the entire year. Wilde was depressed to the depths of his being, and there was little heart in any of his followers. The sixth day brought a respite from the snow—and also revealed that they were now close to Varzi. It was decided that now was the time to split up into small groups, each of which would make for its own town or village and rejoin the partisans when the spring came. The groups dispersed unemotionally and rapidly: for one thing, most of the partisans were accustomed to this sort of winter dispersal; for another, they were far too weak and exhausted for more than a nod and a smile.

Wilde had no farm or town to go to, and decided to make his way south through the snow towards the Allied lines.

As for the three girls, he told them they could join the Varzi contingent. "But it has already left," they told him. "And surely you wouldn't just abandon us in the snow?"

In any case, they were not heading for Varzi, but for Mossago, a small village three miles to the north of the town, where an aunt of theirs had a farm. It would be more comfortable and relaxed than spending Christmas dodging the Fascists in Varzi. Would Wilde accompany them—even although it meant travelling hard all that day if they wanted to reach the farm before the middle of the night?

"I really had no choice," he now smilingly confesses.

Chapter
THIRTEEN

Christmas and Early Spring

DURING the afternoon they bypassed Zavattarello, and in the evening crossed the metalled minor road that led to Varzi close by the turreted castle of Pietra Gavina. Progress was slow and painful, and they moved with caution and spoke in whispers, knowing that they were now in an area where enemy patrol activity was intense. Wilde was startled, therefore, when he heard Giovannina, who was heading the file, say in a loud voice, "*Buona sera.*" In the dusk Wilde could see a German patrol grouped at the far side of a hedge. He ducked down and reached for his P38 revolver. Maria grasped his arm and signalled him to remain still. Reluctantly he did so—and stayed quiet and motionless as he heard the girls agree to walk with the Germans as far as their near-by patrol post.

His mind filled with misgivings, Wilde headed along the road for Mossago, finding his way to the Camporotunda farmhouse from the discreet questioning of passers-by. He wondered what he would say to the girls' aunt by way of explaining both who he was and how her nieces had been delayed.

He knocked at the door, and as it was opened he heard a great burst of laughter. The three girls, together with their mother, sister, three brothers, and various aunts, cousins, and uncles, were sitting by the fire eating chestnuts. They explained that they had not been asked any awkward questions by the Germans, and had managed to make their stay at the post a brief one. Then they had taken a short cut home.

Several bottles of sweet, sparkling wine of their own vintage were produced, and the vast number of womenfolk present came and kissed him on the cheeks. The warmth of the reception, together with contradistinction between his surroundings now and what they had been during the past week, overwhelmed Wilde. He was dazed and speechless.

Someone called, "Cheer up. It's nearly Christmas."

Christmas—and all that word evoked. Christmas at sea, Christmas in barracks, Christmas a year ago in Voghera, and, most of all, Christmas in Sheffield with his family. "Yes," he echoed, "it's nearly Christmas."

It was late now, and Wilde became aware once again of his overwhelming weariness. One of the Camporotunda brothers escorted him to his sleeping quarters. This was an artificial cave, a dugout that lay just outside the village. It was a good place to hide, and not too austere. The walls had been skilfully shored up, and a plentiful supply of hay and straw kept it well insulated from the cold outside. That night, however, Wilde was in no mood—or condition—to appreciate it. He threw himself down on the bed in the corner and slept.

He slept far into the next day, December 16th, and in fact spent most of the following two days sleeping and eating. Then, while at the farmhouse, he began to feel sick and giddy. He shivered and perspired, and the nausea in his stomach was not unlike seasickness. Mama Camporotunda took a long look at him and sent him back to bed. "You've got a face like a Chinaman," she told him.

She was going into Varzi that day, and called at the hospital to see Dr Benzoni. He confirmed the symptoms as jaundice. Because of the shortages in the town, he had no suitable medicines to send back to Wilde, but instructed her to keep him warm and to see that he refrained from fats and alcohol. The diet was rigidly adhered to, supplemented with the prescription of an old farmer who lived at the far end of the village: hot milk with a clove of garlic in it. Whether this helped to speed the cure Wilde did not know, but in any event by Christmas Eve he felt well enough to join the family in their festivities. Alcohol might or might not bring about a relapse, but this was an occasion when doctor's orders were going to be ignored.

Wilde was not the only partisan staying with the Camporotundas. There was Carlo himself, who had been away liaising with the Third Lombardia Division at the time of the evacuation of Varzi, and so had not made the disastrous trek from Capannette di Pej. Shortly before Wilde and his sisters came he had been rounding up stray partisans in the area many of whom were making their way home for the winter and were in need of a few days' respite. There were ten of these fellow-guests on the day Wilde arrived. Fortunately, the dugout was large enough to accommodate them all, and it was as well, too, that there was sufficient food to go round. By Christmas Eve only three were left, the others having continued their journeys home—yet Wilde was almost the only male in the village; the rest had gone into Varzi to drink a few seasonal glasses with their friends before attending Midnight Mass.

"I felt the same homesickness I'd experienced the year before in the via Sant' Ambrogio," says Wilde, "but this time I had an uncanny feeling that the Germans would raid the village during the night. However, being the only able-bodied man in the village, I did not communicate my fears to the others. Instead I ate and drank and joined in the laughter and merrymaking—although my ears were alert for the sound of boots stamping through the snow. But no Germans came, and I chided myself for the foolishness which had prevented me from relaxing and enjoying myself properly.

"Next day I went early to the Camporotunda house for Christmas dinner. This time the Germans did come.

"We were having a pre-lunch drink, and in the middle of it a villager rushed in and said a patrol was entering Mossago. There was no time for the four of us partisans to hide. Equally, we could not hope to get away with pretending that we were innocent villagers. There was nothing we could do but fight.

"The living-room of the Camporotunda house was on the first floor, opening to a veranda. It was from there that we awaited the Germans as they came round the corner of the house—a sergeant and five men, all heavily armed.

"I led the attack by vaulting the balcony rail on top of the man leading the column. The others soon followed. I had the satisfaction of flooring two Germans under me on the frozen cobbles. For a second I sensed that I had fallen badly, and then the weight of another of the Germans came on top of me. There was a pressure on my recently mended arm. It gave a sharp crack, and I was stabbed by a searing pain that ran from wrist to collar bone.

"By the time I scrambled to my feet the fight was over. Three Germans had been killed, and the others raced off into the darkness. We fired after them, but our subsequent search revealed neither bodies nor bloodstains. None of our own party had been hurt—apart from myself.

"It was a pleasant enough victory, but none of us were in the mood for celebrating it. We knew that should reprisals come they would be thorough and ruthless. At the best there would be beatings, the slaughter of cattle, and the burning down of houses and farms. At the worst, the death of the Mossago villagers. But there was nothing we could do but wait—and pray."

As the three corpses were dragged away Wilde returned to the house and was helped off with his coat. Already his arm had swollen to twice its normal size, and he became aware of the terrible waves of pain that surged through it. At first Wilde agreed with Carlo that it was merely a dislocation, but after two fruitless—and agonizing—attempts to pull it back into position Wilde changed his mind and said it must be a fracture of some kind. Once again he was in trouble. As a temporary measure he asked that some wood should be cut into improvised splints and then fixed tightly into place along his arm with a torn-up sheet.

"The only pain-killer in the house was alcohol," says Wilde. "As we sat down to our delayed, and rather sombre, meal I drank myself into a state of mild anæsthesia. It dulled both the pain and thoughts of enemy reprisals."

On Boxing Day Mama Camporotunda again called on Dr Benzoni, explaining how concerned Wilde was in case the break did not set properly. She knew that because of his position in the hospital it was impossible for the doctor to leave town. Equally, because he was well known, Wilde could hardly enter Varzi—indeed, that was why he had not come along on Christmas Eve. Could the doctor not give her something with which to relieve the pain? But the doctor's medical supplies were virtually non-existent by now, and Mama Camporotunda returned to Mossago with no more than a roll of bandage and Dr Benzoni's advice to Wilde to keep his arm as still and straight as possible.

There was no choice but to hope for the best. In fact, the arm was to set quickly and perfectly; and Wilde's intake of pain-killing alcohol brought no adverse post-jaundice effects. His morale was kept high by the perpetual cheerfulness of the Camporotundas, who made it appear that he was doing them the greatest honour in the world by permitting them to house, feed, and nurse him.

Apart from the girls, Wilde found a companion in their brother Ottavio, who was not yet nine years old. The boy would spend hours on end outside Wilde's dugout catching sparrows. He used a trap devised from a piece of wood, a wire loop, and a sprung wire concealed in the snow. The bait was a small square of bread. As soon as a bird was caught Ottavio administered the *coup de grâce* by banging its head against a stone, and he would then pluck it while it was still warm. The little birds were fried over an open fire and eaten whole, bones and all.

The trap usually worked well. One day Ottavio had caught a dozen sparrows, and had put them in a line beside the fire at the entrance to the dugout. As Wilde was about to start cooking them he heard a cry of annoyance. Investigating, he saw that the trap had sprung, but either its loop had failed to imprison its victim or the sparrow had been unusually sprightly—it was perched on the roof of a house with the loop clutched fast in its beak, the rest of the trap hanging harmlessly down. Ottavio shook his tiny fist and shouted, "*Dove via? Viene qui*" ("Where are you going? Come here"), but the bird flew away, the trap still clutched victoriously in its beak. Wilde roared with laugher, and for a while Ottavio was no longer his friend but his sworn enemy!

He grew to like the lad, but was worried by his strong and savage temper. Once they were in the kitchen of the Camporotunda house when Maria started teasing Ottavio. He seized the wicked-looking salami knife that was lying on the table and threatened to stab it into his arm if she did not stop. Thinking he was bluffing, Maria continued her teasing. In a flash two things seemed to happen at the same time—the boy stabbed at his left arm with the knife, and Wilde grabbed at the long cane on the table that was used for mixing *polenta* and brought it down as hard as he could across the lad's bicep. Ottavio dropped the knife and tears filled his eyes—less from the pain than from the shock. Uncharacteristically, he stood meek and silent as Wilde gave him a severe talking to.

To Ottavio the most fascinating of all occupations was that of fighting the Germans. He never ceased to be thrilled by his association with the partisans who came and went, and was continually asking Wilde to tell him of his adventures. Whenever they went for a walk he would ask, "*Dove andiamo? Prendere Tedeschi?*" ("Where are we going? To catch some Germans?").

To catch some Germans. . . . It was a short, if particularly severe, winter, and the month of January made the business of partisan activity a reality once again. Colonel Fiorentini began a series of visits to Varzi, the purpose of which was to demonstrate the power and strength of the German and *fascisti* forces. Wilde's victory the previous October, and the weeks of occupation by the partisans, rankled with him, and inspired him to frequent—and often pointless—acts of vengeance. Sometimes they would take the form of mass arrests and imprisonments; sometimes the wilful destruction of property.

The Camporotundas suffered in this way. On a day when, fortunately, all the family was away in Mossago, the shop near the Municipio in Varzi was broken into by Fiorentini's men. Every item of furniture was removed, the doors were smashed from their hinges, the stock was destroyed and a wide hole knocked in the shop's floor. Broken floorboards and ceiling plaster almost completely filled the cellar beneath. It could have been that their shop was selected by pure chance; on balance the Camporotundas were more inclined to believe that an informer had reported their affiliation with the partisans. The wisest plan, from every point of view, was to keep away from Varzi and help the partisan activities that would soon be getting under way from Mossago.

Inexplicably, there had been no raid or reprisal following the Christmas-morning battle. Wilde's guess was that the survivors had preferred to say that they had been set upon by a large detachment in the hills rather than admit to the ignominious truth. There was, however, an early start to the enemy's patrol activities which had the result of stirring into action partisans who would normally have still been hibernating. From villages higher up the mountain slopes, and from villages and hamlets around Varzi, men began to gather at Mossago. In groups of eight, ten, or a dozen they reported to Wilde, who formed them into the nucleus of a new battalion. There was little active work that could be done for the moment, and Wilde had to content himself organizing sentries and defensive patrols.

It was not until the end of January that his arm allowed him to be fully active again. He moved his headquarters from the dugout to the Camporotunda barn. It was of almost identical construction with the one belonging to Pietro's nephew in Medassino where he had spent his first days of freedom—but its strategic position was quite different. It was perched—seemingly precariously—on a steep, orchard-covered hillside several hundred feet above the village. From its upper storey it commanded a magnificent view of the surrounding countryside.

It was while Wilde was leading his men on patrol that he met one of the partisans who had gone off with Primola Rossa. From him he learned the dreadful story of his old friend.

One day, ski-ing high on the Apennine slopes above the Penice Pass, Rossa encountered a ski patrol of Brigata Nera. Rossa was an expert skier and knew every inch of the mountains. He knew he could dodge the patrol and escape to safety without any difficulty, but since he believed in harassing the enemy in every possible way, he thought he would give them a wearying run for their money before slipping away. And he did—swooping and circling and dodging, allowing the enemy to come close before skimming away over the snows.

Then came disaster.

As he turned, his ski hit an obstacle hidden under the snow. He fell—and broke his left leg. The patrol came up to him, and one of their number, a local man, recognized Rossa as a partisan.

His leg was put into rough splints, and he was taken into Varzi. From there he was hurried to Voghera, where Fiorentini subjected him to a long and brutal interrogation. But Rossa would reveal nothing, and so he was sent to the notorious punishment prison at Cicognola, near Broni, farther down the Po valley. This was the site of the infamous well, the *pozzo di Cicognola*. In it partisans and other political prisoners were kept until they died of starvation and thirst. It was of such a construction that its narrow circumference did not permit a man to lie down, sit, or even lean away from an upright position. In the well a prisoner just stood . . . and stood . . . and stood . . . and died.

Despite his leg in its splints, Rossa was pushed into the clammy, stinking foulness of the well. But they did not leave him there to die—his injury suggested a far more amusing idea. First they offered to spare his life if he gave them the information they wanted about the partisan movement. "No," he replied. "If I die one partisan dies. If I talk many will die."

So they hauled him out of the well and made a mock examination of his broken leg. Said the officer in charge: "Your leg will have to be amputated. Above the knee. We have decided to do it here at Cicognola, where—unfortunately—we have neither a skilled surgeon nor anæsthetics. Of course, if you were to oblige us with the information we require we could arrange for another medical opinion elsewhere. Who knows, it will probably be decided that no operation is necessary, with or without anæsthetics. What do you say?"

Rossa said nothing.

So they cut off his leg.

"The story sickened, then inflamed me," says Wilde, "as it did all the partisans throughout the Oltrepo. It was the signal for a marked increase in activities around Varzi. By now I had between eighty and a hundred men under my command, yet I was not at all anxious to weld them into a division and repeat the events of the previous summer and autumn. Thinking things over during the inactive weeks of the winter, I was now not at all certain that large units with grandiose titles were the most effective way of marshalling partisan strength. I decided to wait and see what the best strategy would be.

"In a way I felt restless. It was all very well biding my time to work out the best way of employing my men, but in the meantime I felt the need for action. I found it by joining up for a week with a group of twelve Czechs I encountered on patrol.

"Like the *mongoli*, they had escaped from a German extra-territorial battalion. They managed to keep themselves smart and clean despite the slushiness of the thaw, and were well disciplined. One of them had a British ·303 rifle, and I begged them to let me have it in exchange for a *mitra.* But its owner would not part with it, although he did lend it to me during a raid on one of the guard posts outside Varzi. It was satisfying to see a sentry in the sights at near-maximum range and fall—presumably dead—at the first squeeze of the trigger. The captured German and Italian rifles we had were far inferior to the ·303.

"After a week the Czechs moved on, away from the Varzi area. They had agreed among themselves that, no matter how attractive a particular location might be, they would keep on the move, travelling from partisan band to partisan band, until they finally caught up with the Allies as they came through the enemy lines. I returned to Mossago."

A few days after the Czechs departed a group of sixty partisans arrived to see Wilde. All were experienced fighting men and had regrouped at Capannette di Pej. It meant that Wilde now commanded a total of about a hundred and fifty men, and since no other plan offered itself he decided to consider the possibility of reoccupying Varzi. Wilde set to work evolving a plan of attack. But the garrison came to hear of the force massed outside the town—and without a shot being fired they simply abandoned the town and withdrew to Voghera!

So once again Varzi changed hands, and once again Wilde was cheered and fêted as the conquering hero. This time his reception was even more hysterical than after the battle of Varzi: the mere mention of Wilde's name, it was said, was enough to send the enemy running away. The return to the town still meant that Wilde's desire for action was unsatisfied, and when he heard that his old friend Falco had collected a group of partisans under his own command in the hills behind Bagnaria he decided to visit the swashbuckling pirate.

He was quite unchanged—except for his name. He had decided that it was bad for security for partisans to use the same name year after year. To set the example, he now called himself Tonka. His highly efficient force, which was doing great work in the area, was called the "Forza Effettiva del Distaccamente Molinari", after a partisan called Molinari, who had lost his life in a heroic battle against the *fascisti*. There were twenty-seven local men attached to it, as well as the *mongoli* who had stayed with Falco during the winter.

Falco introduced Wilde to his second in command, then to a man who, he explained, was officially his number three, but in reality acted as the unit's political commissar. Wilde was astonished on two counts: one, that Falco should be leading what was plainly a Communist detachment; two, that his commissar was the famous Chiri-ci-chi. Falco explained that his Communist affiliations sprang from his admiration of a singularly purposeful partisan leader with whom he had served during the worst of the winter—a man who had managed to provide them with plenty of action during the entire period of what was normally complete inactivity. He admired the man as a fighter, not as a politician. His name was Dino Ricotti, but his current *nom de guerre* was Di Rosa, Falco emphasized. At all events he was certainly well qualified for guerrilla warfare, having been a member of the International Brigade during the Spanish Civil War. He was currently Falco's immediate superior, and seemed to be building a series of small forces, composed entirely of veteran partisans, whom he usually left to wage their own campaigns in their own regions, deploying them against specific targets as the need arose.

The fighting spirit and efficiency of the Molinari partisans attracted Wilde, and he asked Falco if he could join the group for a couple of weeks before returning to his own men at Varzi. Falco was delighted, and when Wilde offered to change his name to Pietro the big man was overjoyed. There was a pause, then Falco, plainly embarrassed, asked Wilde whether he minded not taking command of the Molinari detachment, for it would not be possible to hand over without first asking Di Rosa. Wilde was touched, but assured Falco that he would very much enjoy a spell in the ranks. And so it was arranged, and the two men settled down to an evening of reminiscence.

After a three-day patrol Falco and Wilde returned to camp above Bagnaria to find a messenger with orders from Di Rosa. A large German force was being lured into the mountains around Pozzol Groppo, where one of Di Rosa's other *distaccamenti* had been active. The plan was for this detachment to retreat sufficiently deeply into partisan territory—with the Germans following—where conditions would more than compensate for the enemy's greater fire power. All other partisan detachments were to rally at Pozzol Groppo.

They had time for a quick meal and a couple of hours' rest before leaving for the rendezvous. Di Rosa's plan began by working beautifully. Falco's detachment went into action as soon as it arrived, taking up its position as part of the circle now completely surrounding the Germans. Crouching alongside Falco, Wilde used his *mitra* economically and accurately, feeling almost a small boy's excitement at being in action again . . . hearing once more the bark of machine-guns, the sporadic crackle of rifle fire, and the curiously flat reverberation of exploding grenades.

But the German unit was of a different calibre from the

majority of troops operating in the Oltrepo. These were first-class fighters. Realizing they were surrounded, they dug in and fought back with skill and courage. It was something of a pitched battle, with the fire on both sides heavy and accurate. The partisans were as courageous as ever, but the Germans were unafraid of death and attempted a number of counter-attacks. Casualties were heavy, but at one segment of the circle the Germans managed to weaken the partisan strength. With almost parade-ground precision they manœuvred themselves into this section and fought their way through in a long salient—although with heavy losses. Speedily, but in good order, they retreated towards Voghera. Although the rearguard finally surrendered it fought sufficiently gallantly to prevent any effective pursuit of the main column. "That's what I like about fighting the Germans," said Falco. "They are detestable as people, but the chances are that they'll give you a better fight."

When Wilde returned to Varzi he promised Falco that he would keep in touch, if only to make sure that they took all possible steps to co-operate in the future against the enemy.

No sooner had he arrived than he found he had to go to Capannette di Pej. One of the Allied special-service units operating to the south and west of Varzi had arranged for a parachute drop of arms and supplies on the plateau behind the village. The various partisan groups who would benefit from the drop had asked Wilde to take charge of the supplies and see they were properly distributed.

An hour before the planes were due he had fires lighted at the four corners of the dropping zone. The planes were on time to the second, and the drop was both impressive and strangely beautiful as hundreds of coloured parachutes came floating down with their canisters dangling underneath. They contained arms and ammunition, money and food, and were supplemented by two planes that flew low over the plateau, tipping out their contents bodily. They landed with a series of dull thuds, and turned out to be bales of assorted clothing. Wilde thought he looked a really military figure at last in his khaki battledress and shirt.

Chapter
FOURTEEN

Don Rino Cristiani

BACK at Mossago, Wilde found that things were still quiet except for routine patrols, and although in the early days patrol activity would have offered excitement enough, now he wanted more positive action. He thought he would pay a visit to Domenico and his family at Pozzol Groppo, for his part in the battle there had not taken him near Domenico's farm. When he announced where he was going he ran into unexpected trouble.

Giovannina told him that she did not believe his story: he was going to Pozzol Groppo because he had a woman friend there. There was an argument, and, as so often happens, both of them said things they regretted the moment they were uttered. The climax came when Giovannina drew back her arm and gave him a tremendous smack across the face. "It was with great difficulty that I stopped myself from hitting back," says Wilde. "As it was, the slap seemed to bring us to our senses, and the argument came to an end. But she won her point—for the sake of peace and quiet I agreed to postpone my visit to Pozzol Groppo."

Passing through Mossago at this time was the partisan leader Eduardo, who had sought Wilde's assistance the previous November over negotiations with the Special Air Service party for arms and ammunition. "I have work for you near Zavattarello," he told Wilde. "A special unit has dropped there by parachute. They are Englishmen and much nicer than the people we had to deal with at Bobbio."

Anything was better than the boredom Wilde was now

experiencing at Mossago, and he was soon climbing the mountain tracks with Eduardo. He was a tall young man with a permanently furrowed brow and a vaguely aristocratic look about him. "I'm not certain this Zavattarello business is really your line at all," he said, when they were about three-quarters of the way there. "But I heard you had a row with that fiery young woman, and I fancied you'd like a change of scenery. Frankly, I only asked you on the spur of the moment."

For a moment Wilde was furious—then the humour of the situation came to him. He managed to keep a straight face, and thanked Eduardo solemnly for his thoughtfulness.

The Special Air Service party consisted of two parachutists—an army captain and a wireless operator—and three South Africans who, like Wilde, were escaped prisoners of war. They had been fighting with the partisans to the east before joining up with the SAS men.

It was immediately clear to Wilde that he and the captain were not suited. Remarkably for a man Wilde supposed had been specially trained for this sort of operation, he tried to impose a formal, parade-ground, officer-and-ranker relationship between himself and his men. He was openly scornful of Wilde's command of the Italian language, saying that he had managed to make all the contact he needed with the partisans on the basis of a vocabulary of only thirty words. When he learned that Wilde was just an Able Seaman he became even more remote and supercilious.

Wilde then learned that operating in the area was the American special-service group under the Captain Bill who had visited him in hospital at Varzi some four months earlier. When Captain Bill heard of Wilde's presence he asked him if he would help him with a very important assignment. Wilde was delighted to have an excuse to leave the SAS party.

It appeared that the Americans had somehow managed to capture a German general, whom they were holding near Zavattarello. For reasons Captain Bill was not permitted to explain, the general had to be handed over to another American unit that was operating to the south and east of

Bobbio. Wilde was asked to take charge of transporting the general.

He agreed, and it occurred to him as he did so that so many groups were operating behind the enemy lines—British, American, partisan, and nomadic escaped prisoners of war—that a powerful army could have been formed if only the Allies had taken positive steps to weld them into an organized, unified whole.

On the map the handing-over point for the general was only sixteen miles away, but the need to avoid certain towns and villages and stretches of enemy-dominated roads, together with the natural difficulties of the terrain, meant a journey of about twice that distance.

They set off at dawn the following morning. There were four of them: the general, Wilde, and two of Captain Bill's Italian partisan "irregulars". Wilde's final instructions from Captain Bill were to make sure he sent the two Italians back, and not keep them for his own force—and to call again himself whenever he felt like it.

Their first stop was at Varzi, where they had a late breakfast. The news of Wilde's arrival brought the usual crowd of townsfolk and partisans—the latter now resting on their laurels and lording it as the unchallenged masters of the town. Some of them recognized the general, and quickly attributed to him many of the atrocities that had been committed in the area during recent months.

Immediately an ugly situation developed. There were shouts of "Hang the murderer!" and equally impassioned demands for the partisans to hand him over to the people of Varzi. Wilde recalls that the voices merged together into one vast, animal-like growl, and was appalled at the way a crowd of basically decent, civilized people could dissolve into a primitive mob lusting for blood. It needed all his authority and personality to persuade them to disperse and leave the prisoner to the proper processes of justice.

He was glad to quit the town, avoiding the direct route over Penice and heading south. Towards noon they were passing a small farm which had a lively-looking horse grazing in an adjoining field. It came to Wilde that if they could acquire some form of transport it would enable them to reach their destination without having to spend a night on the road, Sure enough, the farmer had a small trap, which Wilde commandeered together with the horse, and they were soon travelling in style. In point of fact, it was in rather cramped style, since the trap was designed to hold only two people. And when it became clear that the load was too great a burden for the horse, particularly uphill, the escort still found it had a certain amount of walking to do.

A solution suggested itself at the next village, where they saw another horse grazing. Fortunately it was a saddle animal, and Wilde commandeered it with its harness. But a new problem arose: neither Wilde nor the partisans had the first idea about riding. There was a pause, then Wilde looked inquiringly at the prisoner. With a suspicion of a smile the German nodded. Wilde lectured him in both English and Italian on the folly of attempting to escape, and the procession moved off. They arrived at their destination just before dusk, Wilde feeling rather ridiculous. First came the captive, riding imperiously a few yards in the lead. Then came the captors, squeezed together in the tiny trap, with the reins caught up in the *mitra* barrels.

The following evening Wilde was back at Varzi—but again not for long. A message awaited him from Don Rino, who was staying for a few days with his sister, Signora Lazatti, in Bagnaria. The message was in pressing terms, and asked Wilde to come in time for dinner the following day.

Wilde spent the night at Varzi, and arrived at Bagnaria at the appointed hour. He was surprised to see that it was going to be a large party—a fact Don Rino had omitted from his note for reasons of security—and consisted of certain partisan leaders in the area. In addition to Wilde there was Eduardo, four men—Luciano, Sandro, Tritolo, and Tripoli—who had served under him during the previous summer and autumn, and two men he had never met before, Alberto and Mario.

Signora Lazatti provided a memorable meal, and her husband's cellar yielded some excellent wine. The room in which they dined, Don Rino's own room of the first floor, afforded an ideal view for a back-drop: first across the main Voghera–Varzi road, then over the waters of the Staffora and the fields beyond, and finally to the tree-lined ridge of mountains that ran from Pozzol Groppo to Castagnola.

Don Rino said that his purpose in inviting them was threefold. Firstly, he wanted them all to enjoy one another's company in a setting of wellbeing. Secondly, he wanted to show them his new and extensive cache of sten guns, revolvers, ammunition, and hand-grenades which he had secreted "beneath the hooves of the oxen in the stable below". And thirdly he was anxious to discuss with them the situation that would exist in the surrounding valleys as soon as the war against the Germans and *fascisti* was finally won. He was concerned in case there should be outbreaks of violence, and that personal vendettas and old scores should be settled in an atmosphere of rough justice. (Remembering the scene with the general in Varzi, Wilde could well understand the priest's point of view.) Don Rino said he was also worried in case the non-Communist elements among the partisans (Wilde had already noted that none of the priest's wide range of Communist contacts was present) should so fall apart when victory came as to leave it to the well-organized Communists to speak for the entire partisan movement.

The evening continued along these serious lines until about nine o'clock, when—with the exception of Tripoli, who was staying with Don Rino for a further day—the partisans left for their respective homes, camps, or hide-outs. It was a pleasant, starry night, and Wilde enjoyed the winding seven miles of hilly footpaths that led to Mossago. . . .

Less than two hours later a mixed German and Fascist patrol tumbled from armoured troop-carriers and banged at the door of the Lazatti house. Somehow the news of the meeting between Don Rino and the partisan leaders had reached the enemy at Voghera—but the raid had come too late.

Quickly Don Rino helped Tripoli to climb the wall at the back of the courtyard and to escape via a hayloft to the grassy slopes that ran down to the back of the house. Then, taking his time, the priest dressed and went down to the front door, waving to his sister to keep out of sight. As he opened the door the soldiers rushed past him and searched the house. They ignored Signora Lazatti, but Don Rino was placed under arrest.

Sneered the officer in command: "*A Voghera c'e Fiorentini che t'aspetta. Ti fara morire a oncia a oncia*" ("Fiorentini is waiting for you at Voghera. He is going to make you die bit by bit.") And the man who was the idol of the entire Staffora valley was driven away.

For twenty-four hours he was kept in pitch-black solitary confinement in the basement cells of the Castello at Voghera, his hands shackled behind his back. He was given neither food nor drink. The next day he was interrogated by two Fascist civilians, who demanded both information about the partisans and a confession that Don Rino was one of them. He told them nothing. A German Gestapo officer took over the questioning. The priest told him nothing. "Very well," he was told, "now we'll give you to Fiorentini—he'll make you sing."

As a priest Don Rino had a faith to sustain him through humiliations and interrogations that would have broken lesser men. After three days he was taken to Pavia, the seat of the German military command for the district. But still no Fiorentini. For three weeks Don Rino was subjected to almost non-stop, day-and-night interrogations. . . . Questions, questions, questions. . . . Over and over and over again. . . . But he admitted nothing. In the end they sent him to the notorious San Vittore prison in Milan. Block Five, Cell Eighteen, Prisoner Number 2343.

The prison was built on a radial principle, with its six blocks stemming from a central tower like spokes of a wheel. Blocks One, Two, and Three housed "Civil Prisoners", Blocks Four and Six "Non-Dangerous Political Prisoners"; Block Five was reserved for "Dangerous Political Prisoners". Don Rino did not like the word 'dangerous', but thought it a compliment to be placed at the top of the profession—then reproached himself for the sin of pride.

As the German–Fascist cause weakened, the frequency of executions increased. Violence was the only outlet the captors could find for their sense of humiliation and the realization of defeat. They were behaving like madmen, revelling in a final orgy of blood; the dying, desperate gesture of the damned. Occasionally Don Rino was able to administer the Last Sacraments; but more often than not his assistance was limited to hearing Confession and to promising to convey a final message or a scribbled note to a man's family.

Sometimes these notes were smuggled back to the villages. Inevitably they were passed to the partisans operating in the area—a guarantee that the flames of hatred and revenge would continue to burn bright, and that there would be no falling off in determination because the end of the War was near. One such note read:

"*Mamma e Papa,*

Due minuti prima di morire scrivo a voi per dirvi di essere forti, di non piangere e soprattutto di non maledire il mio destino.

Pietro."

"Two minutes before dying . . . be strong . . . do not weep . . . and above all do not rail against my destiny."

With the ending of the winter and the improvement in the weather the desperation of the enemy was reflected in the hard fighting in which the partisans of the Emilian Apennines were engaged. Wilde was pleased at the successes which were being achieved—but depressed that there was nothing worth while happening in the immediate area of Varzi. The influence of the 'professionals'—the British and American special-service teams which had been dropped in the area—was plain to see, but after his experiences the previous summer and autumn Wilde found this style of fighting less satisfying than that of the partisans. For the special units were concerned with sabotage, the partisans with killing the enemy.

As March turned into April it became increasingly clear to the partisans that the War was on its last legs—even if they were unaware of the details of Allied strength and movement.

In fact, the twenty-three German and four Fascist divisions opposing the Allies would soon have the broad Po at their backs. The German Commander-in-Chief, General von Vietinghoff, had already proposed a tactical withdrawal to the line of the river Adige, north of the Po, where his armies could reasonably hope to make a stand of some duration and consequence with the mountains of the Tyrol behind them. But Hitler would tolerate no talk of further retreat, and replied to the general's suggestion: "The Fuhrer expects, now as before, the utmost steadiness in the fulfilment of your present mission to defend every inch of the North Italian areas entrusted to your command."

The Allies had decided to break through the enemy line along the Adriatic flank, bypassing the heavily defended city of Bologna. Their attack was launched on the evening of April 9th, after a heavy air and artillery bombardment. The front line lay along the river Senio, a hundred and forty-five miles from Varzi. Consequently, there was considerable enemy movement through the broad Voghera–Pavia front, which meant, in turn, innumerable opportunities for ambushes. But as the stories came to Wilde they revealed that, while enemy losses were heavy, they would have been much greater if only partisan activity had been co-ordinated and properly disciplined. But there was nothing he could do. . . . Or was there?

For if the partisans had been able to capture Varzi, was it so ridiculous to think now of an assault on Voghera—an assault timed for the very moment when the German defenders there would be at their weakest? When this moment would be, depended on the intelligence they could obtain from Allied headquarters—but what an assault it would be, particularly if it took the form of a general uprising, a vast, unified, final burst of glory involving all the partisans and special units in the entire area.

There was only one person to whom such a scheme, involving as it did information from outside, could be put: Captain Bill. Wilde's enthusiasm was infectious, and the American said he would see what could be done.

Meanwhile Wilde encountered another unusually large American unit in the area, twelve parachutists under the command of a yellow-haired giant known as Captain Bob. This unit was doing its share in the ambushing of enemy motorized and armoured columns and in the destruction of bridges and roads. A few days after the Allies crossed the Senio he received instructions to attempt to immobilize the important railway junction at Alessandria—the focal point of lines running south and east towards the front from Turin and the French border. It meant a journey of some sixty miles from Varzi, and Wilde was invited to accompany the American party. He was delighted to accept—even though it meant a long journey at what might well prove to be a vital moment in partisan activity around Voghera.

The detachment consisted of Wilde, Captain Bob, and five other parachutists. They went loaded down with gelignite, a large supply of detonators, what seemed to Wilde to be miles of wire, and all their normal arms and ammunition. "It was a considerable weight," says Wilde, "and it made progress extremely slow."

Just outside Alessandria they made contact with the local partisans, who told them that they were bedevilled by an armoured train which patrolled between Tortona, Novi, and Alessandria, bombarding all the known partisan positions as it went. "We'll fix the goddam thing for you," Captain Bob promised, adding that they would blow up the lines just as the train crossed them. Wilde looked forward to what promised to be something of a Lawrence of Arabia spectacular.

Unfortunately, however, the train was already on the move when they reached the line—and passed close by their hiding-place. Captain Bob cursed at the lost opportunity, and wondered whether he could prejudice his main mission by waiting for the train to reappear—which might not be for another forty-eight hours. He decided against it, but assured the partisan guide who had led them to the track that once the rails were destroyed the armoured train would no longer be able to come along and bombard them.

Their target was a collection of points that converged

alongside a line of signal-boxes and underneath a trellis of overhead gantries just where all the tracks leaving the town bottle-necked through a narrow cutting. Explosives, carefully placed, could cause an enormous amount of damage.

Look-outs were posted in positions from which they could give covering fire, and to Wilde's surprise he was chosen to help Captain Bob with the actual placing of the charges.

"It was early evening now," says Wilde, "and the dusk gave us a feeling of some security as we came out of cover carrying our heavy haversacks. But we moved cautiously; the spot was of tremendous value to the enemy's transport system, and could well have been heavily guarded.

"But we saw no patrols anywhere along the line. We reached the site, and I began stuffing sticks of gelignite between the gaps in the points. I knew pretty well nothing about high explosives, and, apart from feeling clumsy with the unfamiliar work, I was also a bit nervy handling the stuff. Behind me Captain Bob carefully placed a detonator in each wedge of explosive. This was the most dangerous part of the job, and I was glad when we hurried back to shelter trailing the wires behind us.

"There had still been no sign of the enemy, and in a way I felt that it had all been too easy.

"I watched fascinated as Captain Bob pressed the plunger. . . . There were a number of orange flashes, followed by explosions—and I remember feeling disappointed that the noise was a series of sharp cracks rather than a great reverberation of thunder.

"It was quite dark now, and when my eyes refocused after the flashes I could see that the points and track were twisted and buckled and torn, with some lengths of rail sticking crazily upright in the air. It would be a long, long time before any trains passed that spot again."

Almost immediately sounds of commotion and activity welled up from Alessandria. Quickly Captain Bob ordered: "Let's move. They'll be so busy looking at the points they won't think we might have moved farther down the line." He explained that he'd seen a line of electric pylons which carried the local grid supply, and which crossed the railway lines some six or seven hundred yards to the south. As they ran along the permanent way Wilde realized the wisdom of having carried far more gear in their haversacks than could possibly have been needed for the track.

A few minutes later they were packing their remaining supplies of gelignite around the legs of one of the pylons, lashing them tightly into place with adhesive tape. Again Captain Bob set the detonators, and again they watched the explosion from a safe distance. But either the gelignite had been badly placed or they had not used enough of it—for while one of the pylon's legs was severed and there were large holes in the framework of the others, it remained standing, the electricity cables still intact.

Captain Bob cursed and asked, "What else do we have?" Wilde took from his pocket the two hand-grenades he always carried. Captain Bob nodded and took one.

It was a tricky operation: each had to synchronize with the other as they rushed forward . . . pulled the pins from the grenades . . . stuffed them into the hollow steelwork of the two remaining legs of the pylon . . . then turned, ran, and flung themselves down.

Wilde felt the blast of the explosion rush over his back, but when he climbed to his feet he was annoyed to see that the pylon was still standing. "Anyhow," said Captain Bob as they hurried back to rejoin their comrades, "it sure was fun."

Heavy machine-gun fire was now sweeping the countryside, mostly from the armoured car marooned at the far side of the shattered track. But it was firing at random, and although they needed to move carefully until they were out of range, there was no real danger.

Two days later they were back in Varzi—where Wilde was to prepare for the final, and in a way most dramatic, episode of his life in the mountains.

Chapter
FIFTEEN

The Broken Column

THE Allied offensive now had the Germans reeling. By April 11th Allied troops had crossed the Senio and reached the banks of the Santerno. On April 14th Polish forces took Imola, on the road to Bologna; the New Zealand Division crossed the Sillaro, and the 78th United Kingdom Division gained the important bridge at Bastia, in the centre of the front. Six days later, irrespective of Hitler's orders to the contrary, von Vietinghoff ordered a withdrawal. But it was too late now to organize a policy of mobile defence in depth. During the heavy fighting that followed Bologna was surrounded by the Poles and the 34th U.S. Division. It fell on April 21st, and in the battle the Poles destroyed the 1st German Parachute Division, the cream of von Vietinghoff's troops.

Two days later the 10th U.S. Mountain Division crossed the Po near Ferrara. The 6th South African Division, which had been operating on the left flank of the advance, made contact with the British Eighth Army on its right, thereby encircling several thousand German troops and preventing their retreat.

Meanwhile, back at Varzi from Alessandria, Wilde learned from Captain Bill that the Allied commander-in-chief had given orders for a mass partisan uprising—not only in the Oltrepo, but throughout every inch of Italy of which the Germans and *fascisti* were still in occupation. The date for the uprising: April 25th.

"It was a period of intense activity and excitement for me," says Wilde. "Messages were sent out, and the partisans poured down from the mountains. Our stocks of arms and equipment were now pretty high, and for the first time in the entire partisan campaign there were sufficient supplies to go round. I chose as my own position for the attack a point south of the Staffora, half-way between the river and Pozzol Groppo. It is difficult to say how many men I had under my command, for, apart from the two or three hundred I mustered from the Varzi area, I was also joined by three units who belonged to Di Rosa, but said they'd prefer to operate under me, and virtually the entire male population of Pozzol Groppo and other hamlets and villages in the area. Falco, however, decided to play his part in the attack on Voghera independently.

"It was an impressive army that I had gathered around me, but, unlike the troops that had marched on Varzi, they had never been welded together into one organized unit. Further, with so many non-partisans rushing up demanding guns and bullets, I was very concerned that my men would soon cease to be even a rough-and-ready army, but a hysterical, looting mob screaming out for blood.

"Someone commandeered a white horse from a near-by farm and insisted that I should mount it and lead them to victory in some style. Fortunately it was a docile animal, and my lack of any knowledge of horsemanship did not prevent me from jogging along without too much discomfort or apprehension.

"There was a great deal of noise and cheering and surging forward, but I realized that it was impossible to attempt to impose any discipline. Then Captain Bill came up with the signal to advance. I mounted my horse and led my troops across a narrow bridge over the Staffora, past a now deserted German blockhouse, and into Bagnaria. We must have presented a strange—and probably terrifying—sight: hundreds of roughly dressed men, armed to the teeth, pouring along the country roads.

"The news of the uprising brought with it the joyful peal of church bells, ringing to announce the final victory and to celebrate the glory of the occasion. As we entered Bagnaria I was greeted by the ringing of that very bell I myself had rung with a bullet the previous summer. Suddenly it all seemed very far off and remote . . ."

In Bagnaria Wilde learned that another partisan column had already passed through Bagnaria towards Voghera. He was anxious not to miss the fighting, but realized that he would never catch up if he continued to plod along cautiously on his horse. Luck was with him. Outside the guard post at Bagnaria he found an abandoned German ammunition lorry. He also discovered the German driver, hiding in some outbuildings, terrified that the partisans were going to torture and kill him. Instead he was relieved to learn that Wilde merely wanted him to drive Captain Bill and himself towards Voghera.

Wilde had no worries about leaving his troops behind—he was now certain that even if he had stayed with them as far as Voghera they would have become a rabble, taking orders from no one.

Outside Voghera there was little sense of order. The partisans in the area had surrounded the town, and their offensive, while enthusiastic, was chaotically undisciplined. There was no planning. Various groups advanced on the suburbs independently, firing wildly as they went. For their part, the defenders fought back bitterly and strongly. Dismayed at the ineptitude of the attack, and rather than become members of a mob, Wilde and Captain Bill left the attackers to get on with it in their own way, and merely acted as observers.

"I was depressed and almost heartbroken," says Wilde. "What could have been a glorious final battle was just a wild advance by an army of savages. I felt ashamed.

"The fighting lasted all that day and for part of the morning of the 26th. Then the rains came down in a great heavy, unbroken sheet, and I think this played as much a part in the collapse of the defence as did any specific partisan action."

When Captain Bill and Wilde entered the town they were greeted by wild, chaotic confusion. Wilde saw that it was going to need a strong hand to impose law and order in the town. Coping with the excesses at Varzi had been relatively easy—here the position was magnified a hundredfold.

Wilde's first visit was to the via Sant' Ambrogio, where he was disappointed, but hardly surprised, to find the Bertis' flat at Number One bolted and deserted. Without them there, he could not bear to stay on and watch the riot-like scenes in the town. He would go to Medassino. . . . But as he was about to leave he bumped into Falco.

The latter's partisan unit had remained compact and efficient, and Falco had just received the surrender of a large German detachment. Wilde watched as rifles and machine-guns were piled alongside boxes of ammunition and the German colonel in charge marched up smartly and saluted. Falco did not return the salute: instead he indicated that he wanted the colonel's revolver. Politely the colonel refused, then went into a long speech about the honour of his profession and, most important, the honour of a German officer.

Falco exploded: "*Onore* nothing. There is no such thing as German *onore*. I spit upon your *onore*. Torture and murder are your *onore*. The *onore* of Hitler! I want that revolver." He got it.

News reached Voghera that Mussolini and his mistress, who were *en route* for Switzerland under the escort of a German armoured column, had been captured by a partisan patrol, shot, and strung up head downward from meat-hooks. This information brought renewed jubilation to the people of Voghera. Many collaborators in the town were reduced to a pathetic state of fear, but for the moment there was only one man the partisans were searching for: Fiorentini.

With the crumbling of German military power across northern Italy, partisan prisoners were being released by the hundred. Most of them were able to find speedy transportation to their homes, and in the few days that preceded the final surrender there were many joyful and touching reunions in Voghera. An early arrival was Primola Rossa, in an Italian army uniform with a badgeless forage cap.

Despite his missing leg, and although he had no kind of artificial limb fitted, he refused to have his trouser leg pinned up. The sight of it flapping in the wind was something people soon came to recognize. It acted as a symbol—if any were needed—of the days of occupation, partisan resistance, and Fascist excesses. Rossa's crutch was of unusual design, too. He used only one, slightly less than hip-length, with a spade grip. Rossa was already making light of his infirmity, and from Voghera he made a brief visit to his home at Ponte Nizza before hurrying on to rejoin his partisans. "There are still things to be done," he explained.

Another returning prisoner was Don Rino, who was released from San Vittore prison on April 28th. His main concern was for his parishioners, and he left Voghera with a stern injunction to the partisans to put from their minds all thoughts of vengeance. Justice, yes, he told them. Vendetta—no.

The overall situation changed from hour to hour. On April 27th the Eighth Army had crossed the Adige in the direction of Padua and Venice, and on April 29th two of von Vietinghoff's representatives signed a document of unconditional surrender at Field-Marshal Alexander's headquarters. By May 2nd nearly a million German troops had completed their surrender.

The war in Italy was over. . . . But not quite over for Wilde. There was still the matter of Fiorentini. . . .

When he arrived at Medassino Wilde was given a magnificent welcome. He recalls: "Teresa's father killed his prize fowl and opened his finest bottle of wine. We sat up and talked until about three in the morning, exchanging memories and adventures. Next morning I slept late, and was still dressing when I heard a neighbour hurry in and announce that Teresa and Giuseppe were home. I rushed out of the house, my shirt tails literally flying in the wind, and grabbed the first bicycle I could find. When I reached the via Sant' Ambrogio the front door was open. I almost fell off the bicycle in my excitement, and dashed inside. . . . And there they were.

"The tears just rolled down my cheeks. I was trembling like a leaf, and was hardly able to speak. We kissed and embraced, laughed and cried. It was a scene of complete and absolute joy. For the rest of that day we just sat and talked and talked "

In the days that followed Teresa produced a series of bumper meals, complaining all the while of the amount of weight Wilde had lost because of his active life in the hills. But as time passed a cloud began to spread over their happiness—all three of them knew that now the War was finally over it would not be long before Wilde left Voghera and began his journey home.

Meanwhile Wilde kept a regular check on the happenings in the town. It seemed that, after the first wild enthusiasm and irresponsibility, things were beginning to get back to normal. He looked up many old friends, and re-established contact with Captain Bill, who was now living in style in one of the finest apartments in the town. Wilde made a particular point of visiting Serafina to thank her for the part she played in getting him to Pozzol Groppo—and thus to the partisans.

Then came the news he had been waiting for: Fiorentini had been captured and was in the Castello.

The partisan committee now running Voghera had ordered that their prime enemy was to be kept in solitary confinement with no visitors. But Wilde's authority was still such that there was no question of his not being permitted to see the Fascist colonel. He took Giuseppe with him.

They saw a very old man, his thin white hair untidy, a large bruise under one eye, crouching dejectedly on the bench of his cell. At first he failed to recognize Wilde, until the Englishman reminded him of his imprisonment in the via Cavour, and then of the many times they had clashed, directly and indirectly, over the past months. At the mention of Wilde's imprisonment Fiorentini fell on his knees. "Remember, I never ill-treated you. Remember that." He was a pitiful sight, and for a moment Wilde felt a touch of compassion. . . . Then he remembered the crimes the old man had committed.

The town was bubbling with hate. It was clear that control lay in the hands of the people and in no way with the representatives of the Allied forces, such as Captain Bill, who were trickling into Voghera. There was some conflict, however, as to which of "the people" were in command. The Vogheresi, free after years of subjugation, wanted to run their own affairs for a change, without any interference from outside. The partisans, it was argued, were countrymen from the hills and villages, and therefore not Vogheresi. At the same time the partisans said that they had won the War for the Vogheresi and intended to have their say. Wilde's sympathies were with the partisans, not only for sentimental reasons, but because he realized that, however hot-headed they might be, they were less inclined to embark on a blood bath of vengeance than were the townsfolk.

There would be no arbitrary execution of Fiorentini, the partisans decided. He would be given a "trial of the people". There was little doubt as to the verdict, but a trial by the partisans would serve to retain unity among the various units. For this reason a delegation came to the Bertis' home and asked Wilde to be present at the trial—not only because he would want to be there, but to make certain discipline was maintained, and to prevent squabbling among the different factions. His reputation as a partisan leader, and as an exponent of fair play, was such as to assure that all sides would accept his decisions. On the other hand, what they finally did with Fiorentini was their own business.

The trial was held on the balcony of the Municipio. With Wilde standing beside him, Fiorentini stood in the centre of a group of leading partisans. A man whom Wilde did not know read out a seemingly interminable list of charges. As it went on there were impatient murmurs from the crowd outside the Municipio. The officials themselves began to grow restless, and even Fiorentini shuffled his feet. Finally the list came to an end.

There was the briefest of pauses, then the mob packing the street outside the Municipio roared as one voice, "*Mort' a Fiorentini.*" Wilde looked down. "It was an ugly sight," he recalls. "It was like a pack of starving hounds baying for a trapped fox. They wanted blood. In a way it was understandable. For years they had been oppressed, humiliated, ill-treated, and terrified. During all that time hate had festered and simmered and fermented—and now was boiling over in screaming demand for revenge.

"It was as well that the civilian population down below didn't know one thing—that it had been decided that Fiorentini should not be executed at Voghera, but outside Varzi. For it was with the latter town that the partisans principally associated the Fascist leader.

"I signalled to a small but hand-picked escort, and Fiorentini was returned to his cell, through the crowd of jeering, jostling, spitting people in the streets."

On the morning of May 3rd, at about nine o'clock, Fiorentini began his journey to Varzi in the back of a small open lorry. His wrists were tightly lashed, one end of the rope secured to a bar across the back of the vehicle. His face bore several new bruises. Ten partisans were squeezed into the lorry with him, and at the last moment they were joined by the burly figure of Don Rino. The priest had refused a more comfortable ride in a senior partisan's car (already the trappings of rank were to be seen), partly in the hope of preventing further ill-treatment of Fiorentini, and partly in order to prepare him for the *gran passo*.

It was part of the agreement among the partisans that Fiorentini's trial—more accurately, the reading of the list of his offences and the passing of sentence of death—should be repeated at all the villages through which the column of six vehicles passed. So the long, wearying list was recited at Rivanazzano, at Godiasco, at Ponte Nizza, and at Bagnaria. Wilde feared that each stop, with its terrible statement of crimes, would provoke a lynching. The crowds pressed hard against the lorry, shouting threats and curses. "*Mort' all'assassino, al sanguinario!*" was the most widely yelled slogan. There were shouts for Don Rino and the partisans to climb down from the lorry and leave Fiorentini as a clear target for the rocks, stones, and cudgels that seemed to be in everybody's hands. Wilde wondered what would happen if the crowds did attempt to take Fiorentini by force—would they have to protect the Fascist by cracking open heads with their *mitra* barrels? Fortunately Don Rino's cloth—together with his steadfast refusal to budge an inch from the prisoner's side—just saved the day. Indeed, the priest even managed to persuade the procession to stop twice at farmhouses along the route in order to obtain a glass of wine for the prisoner.

At Varzi there was still a sense of celebration and reunion. Old friends were meeting for the first time in months or years. Primola Rossa was there, as was Falco, and Wilde was acutely aware of the fact that this time his meeting with his partisans might well be the last. He thought it was fitting that Don Rino should also be there: for his three principal comrades to be together with him for the final drama.

The trial on the steps of the mortar-scarred Municipio followed the pattern of the others, with the same threats and ugly atmosphere. Again the cry went up, "*Mort' a Fiorentini*," and again the prisoner was taken down to the cells.

A few minutes later, walking across the square, Wilde heard his name called. It was Primola Rossa, who was involved in a conversation with a British Army major wearing parachutist's uniform and regulation beret. How he came to be in Varzi he did not explain, but he had witnessed the trial at the Municipio and felt it his responsibility to have Fiorentini transferred to the authority of the Allied forces who would be occupying the area within the next few days. He was trying to force his views on Primola Rossa, and the partisan turned imploringly to Wilde.

"You see this," he said, pointing to his flapping trouser leg. "Tell him—and tell him to leave Fiorentini to us."

The major turned to Wilde, wondering why he was being transferred from one Italian to another. "I saw you up there on the balcony," he said in his halting Italian. "What do you have to do with all this?"

"I am an Able Seaman of the Royal Navy. A submariner," Wilde replied in English, enjoying the major's open-mouthed incredulity. "The claim these men make on Fiorentini is absolutely just in terms of the atrocities he has committed." He went on to summarize some of the crimes of which the

Fascist was undoubtedly guilty, then satisfied the major's curiosity about his own presence there.

The major asked, "Are you in charge of this town?"

"Not really, but I suppose I could be if I wanted to."

"And you have no wish to exert your authority and endeavour to save this man's life, or at least guarantee formal proceedings against him as a war criminal?"

Wilde shook his head.

"Very well," said the major, "I might as well look the other way and make tracks for Voghera. I might be of more use there. You are clearly able to judge the present situation far better than I can. Good luck." With that he drew himself to attention, saluted Wilde, and made off through the crowds. Wilde beckoned to Rossa, who had been viewing the proceedings apprehensively, and told him the execution could go ahead as planned.

Wilde returned to the Municipio to be told that Fiorentini had been asking to see him. "I am hungry," he said. "I have had nothing to eat today."

"You'll soon be eating lead," Wilde replied, turning on his heel and leaving the cell. The brutality of the remark came to him as soon as he uttered it, but he could not bring himself to return to the cell.

The partisans were now pouring into Varzi in a steady stream. Many were men who had fought in or around the Staffora valley as part of Wilde's Aliotta Division or under the Communist Lombardia leadership. Others came in from Voghera, men whose service had been in other parts of the mountains or along the marshes of the Po. Some of these latter resented the local possessiveness in respect of Fiorentini, and several wine-loosened tongues blustered criticisms and threatening challenges. Wilde did not think they would prove a problem, but Primola Rossa asked him if he would take charge for the last time, and use his authority to make certain that good order and discipline were maintained. He was not, he stressed, asking Wilde to take any direct part in the execution: that was a job for Italians "to cleanse the hands of the nation".

So it was that Wilde organized police patrols from among the Varzi partisans, and saw that trusted men lined the streets to hold back the throng as the lorry left the Municipio. Progress was slow because of the crowds who wanted a last look at their hated enemy. Wilde's patrols made certain they did not follow farther than the town's limits where the procession turned down a local road towards Pietra Gavina and Zavattarello.

The Italian sense of the dramatic had determined the precise spot for Fiorentini's execution: the bend in the road where Alfieri, then the three partisans shot in reprisal, had died.

Fiorentini carried himself with dignity, and Wilde could not help but admire him. The *belva umana* ("the human wild animal") was wearing an ill-fitting blue battledress and a dirty grey shirt, his white hair falling loosely over his face. For a few minutes he walked up and down with Don Rino, who was wearing his full clerical robes—for the first time in an essentially partisan setting. As they walked the priest heard Fiorentini's confession. He told Don Rino his last wishes, and asked him particularly to send his love to his old mother. Then he turned to the partisans and said out loud "*Ho sbagliato*. I have sinned. . . . And what I am about to receive I have well and truly merited."

By this time the execution squad had been chosen from the hundreds of men lining the road, all of whom had surged forward in an effort to be selected. Wilde had had to use all the authority he possessed to maintain discipline. Even the men he had selected were equipped with a wide variety of weapons for their task—rifles, sub-machine-guns, and revolvers were all in evidence—and one had no gun at all, and borrowed Wilde's revolver before he could join the firing-squad. Wilde noticed two men trying to edge themselves to one side of the firing-squad in order to be able to throw grenades (one had a German stick-bomb, the other a British hand-grenade) at Fiorentini when the order to fire was given. He sent them packing.

Fiorentini was offered a cigarette and a glass of wine. As he stood smoking Primola Rossa came up, leaning on the spade grip of his crutch and from time to time shifting the strap of his *mitra*—he had already made it quite clear that he intended to be the senior member of the firing party.

Soon the cigarette was finished, and Fiorentini was told to step from the roadway and take his stand at the execution spot, the grass verge at the edge of a field.

"*Fucilazione alla schiena*," Rossa commanded—an order for him to be shot in the back.

For the first time the old man showed emotion. Horrified, he turned to the crowd. "Don Rino," he called, "I implore you. Persuade them to shoot me in the chest."

The priest turned to Rossa. "Angelo . . . please."

Rossa nodded and walked over to Fiorentini. In a tone of grudging respect he asked if there was anything else he wanted. The Fascist shook his head—but as Rossa walked back to join the line of the firing-squad he called out, "Let me give the order for my execution."

"No," said Rossa. "That would be too much." Don Rino argued with him, but the young partisan was stubborn.

At this point Wilde intervened, asserting his authority for the last time. Giving his final order as a partisan commander, he said, "What he wants is perfectly all right."

There was silence. As before, no one questioned his command; it was all part of the legend of infallibility that had grown up around him. Rossa looked disappointed—but there was never any question of his being rebellious.

Before minds could be changed Fiorentini called, "*Squadra*." Then: "*Pronto*," bringing them to some semblance of attention. There was a brief pause as he opened his battle-dress jacket and held it open, uncovering his chest. He drew himself upright, and for a second a sort of serenity came to his face. "*Viva l'Italia! Fuoco!*"

"The assortment of weapons barked into life," says Wilde. "It was a sound that, as always, gladdened the ear—but on this occasion saddened the eye. Death was certainly quick. Justice had been done—as was proper. But fighting in the mountains is one thing; watching a man being executed is another. I had no doubts about the correctness of Fiorentini's sentence—yet I would rather have not been there to watch its being carried out. I felt a deep remorse, and although I am not religious I found myself praying in thanks that the War, with all its killing within a nation divided among itself, had finally come to an end."

Quickly the partisans lifted the body of Fiorentini back into the lorry. He was driven to the cemetery at Varzi and buried, the graveside ceremony being conducted by Don Rino. There had been talk of displaying his body in the manner of Mussolini's, but the priest forbade any such action.

For Varzi it marked the end of an era. The little town would long bear the physical and mental scars of the struggle. Wilde hoped that the feeling of bitterness and hatred would die now that Fiorentini was dead. He was not to know that the bend in the road between Varzi and Pietra Gavina would mark something more: a positive step towards ending the recriminations of the past and building towards a united future.

For the people of Varzi, aided by the partisans who had fought for them, and led by Don Rino who had both fought and prayed, decided to erect on the site of the vendetta a memorial to all four men who had been executed there. The names of Giovanni Ballerini, Stefano Fiori, and Arturo Giannozzi were inscribed on a marble tablet, together with a dedication written by Don Rino which spoke of their "serene dedication to justice and to liberty". At the foot of the tablet was added the name of their executioner and subsequent victim: Giovinezze Fiorentini.

The tablet was fixed to the pedestal of a stone column that rose to about five feet. Its top was sloping and uneven, as though it had been cut through. It was a form of memorial not uncommon in that part of Italy, to symbolize a life cut off violently or in its prime.

It was placed at the exact spot where the four men had stood and died. Today, as the visitor, inhabitant, or former partisan passes by, he can still see the broken column that marks just four of so many lives.

Epilogue

"FOR me too," says Wilde, "it was the end of an era. It represented only a few months in my life. An episode. An interlude. Yet, as I alone could know—and was not fully to realize until much later—it was a period of my life that was to influence all that followed.

"The War was over. What was done was done. Now I had to think of the future, of my return to England; even though nothing could ever be the same again.

"First, however, there were farewells to be made: to the splendid, fiery Falco; the intense Primola Rossa; the magnificent Don Rino. Most of all, to Teresa and Giuseppe in the via Sant' Ambrogio, where I spent a last few, sentimental days."

Others came and went across the blurred horizons of those days. The Morinis prepared a Gargantuan farewell banquet at Medassino. He heard from his comrades that legal proceedings were being prepared against all local war criminals and members of the Brigata Nera. Don Rino was an active and prominent member of the case for the prosecution—a man whose word no one would question. But the dramatic news that reached Wilde just before he left Voghera was that the priest had not been making an idle threat against Americano over the shooting of the German prisoners. Don Rino reported the incident, and some months later the Communist leader was sentenced to eighteen years' imprisonment.

A happier item of news was that one of the girls from Pozzol Groppo was to marry one of Wilde's former *mongoli*—the man, Nicolai, who came from Baku, in the Caucasus.

But Wilde's main concern was with the Bertis. There was a thanksgiving service held in the church of San Giuseppe, round the corner in the via Plana. Wilde accompanied the Bertis to it, and afterwards he and Giuseppe talked on into the small hours. Giuseppe assured him that neither he nor his wife regretted anything they had done. Imprisonment had not been too bad . . . it was in a good cause . . . they would do it again. . . . After their first few weeks in the Castello it had become clear that Fiorentini had found other subjects for his displeasure, and the remaining months in Voghera and Milan were dreadful only because Giuseppe was separated from his wife. . . . And so they talked, each aware that when the moment for parting came it would need to be cruelly abrupt.

And so it was. On the following day orders arrived for all Allied personnel to report to Milan. "The trains were running again," says Wilde, "and as mine clanked and chugged out of the town I tried to shut my mind to both the past and the future."

From Milan Wilde was flown first to Siena and then to Naples. There he was sent to the transit camp, where the first thing that happened to him was to be sprayed with DDT!

He recalls: "I felt strangely ill at ease in that transit camp at the foot of Mount Vesuvius. There were many reasons for this. For one thing, I felt embarrassed at having to queue for meals . . . was uncomfortable keeping the fixed hours of an imposed discipline that was not of my own making . . . found I suffered a terrible claustrophobia in the confines of a camp . . . and, worst of all, was so accustomed to speaking and thinking in a gesticulating Italian that English came to me only with difficulty.

"One night I climbed as high as I could up Mount Vesuvius and watched the lights of Naples twinkling below me. This, I felt, was my true element—free and unfettered in the mountains. It was with great regret that I dragged my feet back to camp."

During the week he was there Wilde was subjected to a series of de-briefings, each of which he resented more than the one before. He felt that he was being treated as a suspect enemy, not an Allied serviceman who had done his bit to serve the common cause: a feeling emphasized by the fact that the questioning was done by a couple of South African officers whose interest was remote and disinterested.

"I just couldn't fit into the life and routine," says Wilde. "I tried to focus my thoughts on home . . . on Sheffield . . . my family . . . Doreen, my fiancée. But nothing was real any more. I had left reality behind in the mountains. There was no future, and the present was a vacuum."

After a week Wilde was told to report to the *Empress of Scotland*—another serviceman among the thousands being sent home. He made friends—as far as he was able—with the crew, and for the first time since leaving Voghera began to feel relaxed as he talked in the once familiar atmosphere of a messdeck.

They docked at Liverpool on June 2nd, 1945. Still dazed by what appeared to be the unreality of it all, Wilde caught a train to Gosport and reported to H.M.S. *Dolphin*, the submarine depot. When he reported to the Drafting Cox'n's office he gave his name, rank, and number, and was asked, "What boat?" When he replied that his last boat was *Sahib* he was told, "That's funny: the rest of your lot went through four days ago." The 'system' had not appreciated that he was anything other than an ordinary returned prisoner of war.

On Monday, June 9th, Wilde arrived home at Sheffield. "I was excited now and agitated," he recalls, "but the more emotional I became the more difficult it was for me to speak English. It was to take many weeks for me to be able to describe anything in detail in my native tongue."

As Wilde's own home was a long way from the station, he called first on his fiancée. Her parents told him that she was in bed, tired after the long hours she worked at a local aircraft factory, where she was employed as a welder on fuel tanks for Spitfires and Mustangs. But he was given permission to go to her room and wake her.

"I knocked at her bedroom door," he recalls, "and without awaiting a reply walked in. I stood by the side of the bed and gazed down at the sleeping figure that had waited for me so patiently and steadfastly. Then a great sense of sadness came over me. For some reason I experienced a great, indefinable sense of loss.

"Doreen woke up, and I started muttering in Italian. Then I groped for words to say in English, but it was so difficult that I abandoned the attempt. This was the first time in years that I had been in a house that either had no fears for me or memories of fears—yet still I felt remote and aware of some unreality. It is not an emotion I can easily describe. I left the room and went downstairs, where her parents and two sisters were waiting with a cup of tea.

"It was embarrassing in the extreme to have a group of people hanging on my every word, especially when those words were so difficult to utter. I was relieved when Doreen came downstairs, ushered the others from the room, and we were left alone. I was still nervous, and my tongue seemed several sizes too big for my mouth, but as I calmed down the words came more easily and my fears dissolved. As soon as I became excited again I would lapse back into Italian.

"We made plans to be married. I felt that I needed some sort of anchorage. It was vital to me, since I still felt an overwhelming urge to get away from things—to return to the mountains—and I thought that marriage would give me a more relaxed stability."

And so it was that Wilde married. "I remained mixed up for a long time," he says. "I was easily upset, would fly off the handle at the slightest little thing—lapsing into a combination of English and Italian. Fortunately, my wife seemed to understand how difficult things were for me, and was very patient."

When his leave, which included his honeymoon, was over Wilde reported back to *Dolphin*. None of his former shipmates was there. No one knew him, or knew his history, and he was glad—he felt he could not bear a great series of explanations that would bring back so many memories. When he was ready he would reminisce. In the meantime he preferred to shut his mind to Italy and get on with the routine jobs of a submarine depot.

"One evening," says Wilde, "I did start thinking about

Voghera and the Bertis, about the campaigns in the mountains, and the battles won and lost—and suddenly I felt relaxed. I realized that for some reason I had been ashamed of my escapades, but when it came to me that I had done absolutely nothing to be ashamed of a great feeling of ease and relief came over me."

Wilde got more into the swing of English life. In 1946 he was demobbed, and now came the need for a new adjustment—to civilian life and behaviour. After his demob leave he obtained work in a garage. But it did not appeal to him, and he left.

His next job was as a tram conductor in Sheffield. This he did not find too unpleasant: he enjoyed meeting people, and was allowed to get on with his job without a foreman breathing down his neck. "One day, however, I was reported for having on the upper deck of my tram a man who was travelling without a ticket. What, I was asked, did I have to say about it? The answer was immediate, and came as a tremendous relief to me, the great lifting of a burden:

"I'm going back into the Navy."

"I talked it over with my wife, who was still being subjected to some rough times from me because of my moods and restlessness. She understood and agreed—and so I signed on again."

Wilde reported to the shore base, H.M.S. *Drake*, and requested to return to submarines. For some reason this proved difficult, but finally he was transferred to the submarine depot, *Dolphin*. Now came a moment of magnificent irony. The Able Seaman who had led a brigade of partisans through months of fighting in the Italian mountains, organizing them into a disciplined, crack unit which inflicted many notable defeats on the enemy—failed his examination for promotion to Leading Seaman!

He still did not talk about his Italian adventures to his messmates, and it might all have passed into the anonymity of history but for the fact that he was drafted to the depot ship *Maidstone* in 1947, and there bumped into John Bromage, his commanding officer aboard *Sahib*. Where had Wilde been? What had happened to him after his capture? Did he finish the War in a German prisoner-of-war camp? . . . Slowly Bromage got the bones of the story from him.

As a result of this meeting Wilde became, on November 29th, 1947, the recipient of one of the last decorations awarded for services during the War—the British Empire Medal "for organization of partisan activities".

He remained in the Navy for a further five years. During this time he did succeed in passing for Leading Seaman, and finally took his discharge with the rank of Acting Petty Officer.

Time had played its part. He was now settled and relaxed, absorbed into the domestic scene. He took a job as a telephone engineer with the Post Office, then moved into industry. Today he still lives in Sheffield, works as a carbon and graphite inspector, and is the father of two children, a boy and a girl.

To look at him he is a plain, ordinary, man-in-a-crowd Yorkshireman, with a round face and a small, slightly flattened nose that suggests he once did a bit of boxing.

Look a little closer and there is some vague, indefinable suggestion of the Italian about him, and when he speaks Italian—with a now rather rusty Vogherese accent—his hands come into play, and he bubbles and bounces into a completely different personality from the dour, matter-of-fact Yorkshireman.

"Inevitably," he says, "there are moments of nostalgia. Some corner of my heart will always remain in Italy, and I shall have memories of victories won and the men and women who helped me win them. It is good to have memories of which one can feel proud, even though they are sometimes tinged with regret that one did not achieve more, accomplish greater deeds."

James Frederick Wilde—the ordinary, undistinguished, average man. Until that Saturday in April 1943 when *Sahib* was sunk and he was catapulted into the series of events that led him to become a partisan commander in the mountains of north-west Italy. And ended at a bend on the road from Varzi to Pietra Gavina, where now stands a broken column.